The
Way
of the
River

The
Way
of the
River

*Adventures and Meditations
of a Woman Martial Artist*

BK Loren

THE LYONS PRESS
GUILFORD, CONNECTICUT
AN IMPRINT OF THE GLOBE PEQUOT PRESS

The Lyons Press is an imprint of the Globe Pequot Press

The essay "Eye of the Storm" was previously published in slightly different
form in the anthology *Women on the Verge,* edited by Susan Fox Rogers
(St. Martin's Press, 1999).

Library of Congress Cataloging-in-Publication Data
Loren, BK, 1957–
The way of the river : adventures and meditations of a woman
martial artist / BK Loren.
p. cm.
ISBN 1-58574-301-1
1. Loren, BK, 1957.   2. Women martial artists—United States—
Biography.   3. Martial artists—United States—Biography.   I. Title.

GV1113.L67 A3 2001
796.8'092—dc21
[B]   2001018646

Printed in the United States of America
2 4 6 8 10 9 7 5 3 1

For Lisa Cech
with deepest gratitude

CONTENTS

Author's Note

Though I speak predominantly—almost exclusively—of Chinese martial arts throughout this book, I do not mean to imply that Chinese martial arts are the only or the best martial arts. They are simply the branch of the study that has held my interest over a period of three decades.

I prefer the term "martial arts" to "wushu," "gong fu," "karate," or any other umbrella term, however, because other arts—Shotokan, kendo, kempo, tae kwon do, hapkido, and aikido, to name a few—have also informed my understanding of martial arts as a whole. Although my formal studies of these arts is limited, I have exchanged knowledge and theory with other teachers of these systems and certain aspects of these arts have no doubt worked their way into my routine workouts and my theory of martial arts as a whole. I will admit, from the outset, to having a bias against martial arts schools that claim that the study of one art is preferable to an eclectic approach. I thank my friends and colleagues for their open-minded positions regarding the arts.

The
Way
of the
River

EYE OF THE STORM

The gums are soft and remain.
The teeth are hard and fall out.
—Lao Zi

I. TEETH

Since I hadn't gotten to "multiple opponents" yet, what happened that night in Los Angeles was a surprise. All high school kids have at least one reputation for something, and I had two. The first was for being interminably calm. My friends had great fun with me. They'd toss insults at me or pull practical jokes. My chair was yanked out from under me at lunch several times, and whenever I gave a speech in Basic Communications, my buddies would throw things at me when the teacher wasn't looking. They'd even make up annoying stories like, "Lucy Billings is telling everyone, including the principal, that you were the one who set the toilet paper on fire in the girls' bathroom."

"Oh, that's funny." I'd laugh. "I'll talk to her about it later."
I was weird, imperturbable, boring.

Even though I didn't like football games (getting all riled
up for the good team, cursing the bad), my friends talked me
into attending one game. It was uneventful: the boys crashed
their helmets together, I said "rah," and my friends and I began
our walk home.

Walking home at eleven o'clock at night in Los Angeles
was always a little uncomfortable, but it was better than being
escorted by parents. Besides, the hip city was still oozing with
the love and peace of the sixties. Multicolored VW vans spew-
ing incense and pot smoke cruised the boulevards, and James
Taylor and Carole King serenaded us into a laid-back, termi-
nally cool generation, on the surface.

Beneath the surface, however, there was racial tension,
tension between men and women, tension between rich and
poor, tension between one high school and the next, tension
between gangs. So when Joey Chavez, Billy Carlisle, and their
friends pulled up behind us in Joey's low-rider Impala, my
friends and I knew we were in trouble. When we heard the engine turn off and the doors slam, I remained calm. "Just keep
walking," I said. "They're not going to hurt us."

Then Joey's hand appeared over Debbie's shoulder. He held
her tightly to him as he swaggered, his face real close to hers,
his free hand tracing her jawline. "Leave me alone," she said,
but she was too scared to move or push him away. I watched

as he forced a kiss on her, and she drew back as hard as she could. "I hate you, Joey," Debbie said, and Joey was, for the moment, satisfied with his damage. He left Debbie alone. But Billy turned his eyes toward me. He put his arm around me and started to lean in. I turned out of his hold. Baffled at his clumsiness, he came back at me, this time thrusting his arm around my neck so his hand landed inside my shirt. I turned out again, and it became clear that it was my maneuver, not his clumsiness, that allowed my escape. This irritated him. He locked eyes with his friends, and Billy came at me with both hands from the front while his friends descended on me from every other angle. They grabbed my shoulders, held my arms, and forced me to the ground, four guys, one girl.

I'm not certain of the details of the next few moments. This is all I know: at the end of the skirmish, I was left standing and they were left lying on the ground. Billy was bleeding profusely from the nose.

My friends had already deserted me. I could see them in the distance; they were calling me, and I knew I should run. But I didn't. I stayed there and delivered an enraged lecture. The guys ignored me. They were concerned only with helping their bleeding friend. But my rage had already ignited. I picked up a rock and threw it at them, hard. They looked up. Joey said, "That's a bitch." Then he pulled out his switchblade, and his friends followed.

It took the blade to get me to run, and I ran. I ran faster

than they did. I met up with my friends, and we ran toward a light glowing in a lower-level apartment. When we reached that light, the guys gave up the chase.

It was L.A., land of peace and love. But when we knocked on the door, frantic and tattered as we were, a woman peered at us through her blinds but would not open her door or make a phone call for us. We tried a few other doors and found the same silence. We were thirteen-year-old girls. We walked the rest of the way home huddled together.

That night I earned my second reputation. I was imperturbable—to a point. Joey and Billy had reached that point.

II. GUMS

The sun rises like a huge, humpbacked animal above the arid desert floor. A visible heat wave forms on the horizon, a mirage. Out of the mirage steps a man. He is interesting to look at. His loose cotton pants are held up by a rope tied around his waist. His shirt hangs from his shoulders, and his hat is tattered. He wears no shoes, and he has been walking a long time. He has a look of deep confusion on his face. He seems fatigued. Flute music plays a few minor notes. If you recognize the tune, you will know it is loosely based on a traditional Japanese song. The man and the image swell into your living room. If it is 1973, you cannot escape them. If you recognize the man, you know he is American. He introduces himself as Kwai Chang Caine. If you recognize the name, you know it is Chinese. If you recognize the actor, you know he is David Carradine. "I am Caine," he will say one hundred times in your living room throughout the next few years. He will meet many people in the Old West. He will flatten them reluctantly but efficiently with his kung fu.

This is American martial arts in a nutshell: a loosely based Japanese tune, an almost Chinese name, an American actor, a confused look, a trend.

After I defended myself against Joey and Billy, my friends asked me if I was some kind of "black belt," but the notion confused me. Sifu Liu, my first teacher, taught me various styles of Shao-Lin gong fu (also spelled kung fu). He considered the colored-belt ranking system an American device, created to make martial arts more palatable to a culture that too often relies on external validation and homogenization. He did not hand out belts; if a student asked him why more than once, he would ask that student to leave the *kwoon* (Chinese martial arts studio).

At the heart of what he was teaching, belts could never have mattered. His lessons sometimes consisted of asking us, his students, to stand in one position for up to an hour. Stillness, he said, was the heart of martial arts. In that stillness, labeled hierarchies vanished. Power turned to water; strength looked like yielding. His teachings flipped my notion of the world upside down, never to be flipped upright again. They changed, forever, the lens through which I viewed the world. There were even moments when I felt sure I was looking through no lens at all. I was, for those moments, simply seeing the world.

You have no doubt seen tricks of the martial arts trade. I'm not talking about breaking boards and bricks; I'm talking about the circus tricks: a man stands in one place and ten men cannot move him; five men put all their weight on a spear and two arrows placed in the hollow of a woman's throat, but as the men press, the arrows snap, the spear cracks in two, and the woman remains unscarred, even undented. You might even have seen Bill Moyers's special on alternative healing. A segment of that series portrayed qigong practitioners in China. Bill Moyers watched as a man stood at the center of a circle of people. The people ran at the man forcefully from all directions, but they fell about three feet away from him as if they had run smack-dab into a brick wall. No wall was visible. The man in the center did not move with any apparent force. Bill Moyers said to the audience, "Is this a hoax?" Moyers sat no more than six feet from the spectacle taking place and said he could not see any means of trickery taking place.

The friends with whom I viewed this show laughed.

When Bill Moyers asked the martial artists to what they attributed their "powers," they answered, "*Qi* [also spelled *ch'i*]." My friends laughed again. I tried to explain that qi is energy, like electricity, and like electricity, it can be harnessed and directed. I said, "It's what acupuncture is based on, and acupuncture works on animals, so there's not much room for a placebo effect." However, like a Zen koan, qi cannot be understood by the intellect, and my buddies doubted me. They begged for a demonstration, but as usual, I produced nothing. In my life I have had little opportunity to snap spears with the tender part of my throat, and if ten people tried to push me off balance, I'd likely walk away and let them push each other. But, for several reasons, I have virtually no doubt that the events depicted were real.

I also have little doubt that admitting the existence of qi would threaten some of our most basic cultural beliefs. I remember a time when Sifu was sparring with an advanced student who happened to catch him in the jaw with a solid punch. The student stopped sparring and began apologizing profusely. "Keep on, keep on," Sifu called, unfazed by the blow. The following day, the guy came to class claiming that his knuckles were sore. At first I imagined this to be just idolatry, the student's starry-eyed gaze at the master. It bothered me, however, that Sifu had sustained no visible injury. He did not seem to be sore, and though the sound of the strike landing on Sifu's jaw had produced an audible crack, there was no bruise, no visible damage.

Likewise, after years of study with Sifu and other martial arts teachers, I developed an odd kind of "strength" that has stayed with me to this day. Recently, on a whim and without having practiced external martial arts regularly for many years, I attended a Contact! class (a takeoff on tae bo that includes hitting a heavy bag). Though in my early days as a martial artist, I was almost always the only woman in the class and usually the youngest, here I was the the oldest, and although I was not the only woman, I was the only woman without washboard abs and bulbous biceps. One man wore a Thai boxing T-shirt and looked very strong from a distance. I was ready to swallow my pride, feel the effects of my aging, and tap feebly at the heavy bag in front of me. After we stretched our bodies as Madonna sang "Like a Prayer," the teacher demonstrated a series of punches and asked us to follow. I focused on the shiny black bag, which stood on a heavily weighted base, and I began striking. When the teacher called, "Stop," I looked up. The other students were staring at me. While punching, I had moved my bag from the back row to the front, clearing a path as I hit. A friend who was watching me through the plate-glass window said the bag "jumped" across the floor as I struck it.

I know I am not strong enough to effect that sort of power. But the same people who loosen lids on jelly jars for me do not make the heavy bag move that way when they punch it.

≈

As I began writing this book, I did not intend to record any of my "victories" or "losses," because they are irrelevant. In fact, I don't believe I was victorious or that I lost anything in any sparring match at any time. Rather, each sparring session taught me to see the world differently. My cultural blinders gradually fell away, and I learned that who prevails in any physical confrontation has less to do with muscle mass and gender than we tend to believe. Imagine the change in our world if this knowledge ever got into the hands and minds of the public at large, if they believed it, indeed, if they *knew* it.

The difference martial arts made in my life, however, has everything and nothing to do with self-defense and the ability to punch a two-hundred-pound bag and move it across the floor. The origins of Chinese martial arts have their roots in Buddhism, the tenets of which do not allow a person to harm another being (which is why, early on, martial arts were never to be taught to non-Buddhists). In this vein, the arts I have studied all teach that the only force that can be used against an opponent is equal to the amount of force coming at you from that opponent. There is no occasion to "harm" another person; there is only the occasion to give back to your assailant the harm he is attempting to force on you. It's like a Zen koan "What is the sound of one person fighting?" In any sparring match, there is always only one person fighting; the other relaxes and returns the violent intention to the sender.

In order to do this, a person must be utterly in the moment. There is no time to look at the scoreboard. You look away, you lose. The second you jump ahead or fall back in time, you are reminded of the present in a very solid, physical manner. So you learn quickly that the present is the place to be. After years of practice, you eventually begin to live this way by habit, and your world changes: there seems no past and no future, only a succession of events taking place in the very expansive place called the present. You begin to own your own life.

III. MOUTH

Sifu said I had failed the evening I defended myself against Joey and Billy. I had not failed miserably. It was just that things could have been done better.

He explained to me that he had taught me both styles of martial arts, "hard" (force meets force) and "soft" (circular motions, the cultivation of qi.) He said, "'The teeth are hard and fall out. The gums are soft and remain.' But you need your whole mouth to digest anything substantial."

His lingo translates to this: in martial arts, the gums are the internal systems—bagua, xing yi (the qi-based disciplines), and the soft styles (including many forms of gong fu); the teeth are the external systems—tae kwon do, Mike Tyson's unique, toothy method of boxing, the hard styles based almost entirely on physical strength, speed, and technique. Somewhere between the soft and the hard lies a place where neither is dominant and both are present. The full mouth is more powerful than qi or fists alone, but it takes a long time to learn to use the hard and the soft equally well because they cancel out each other. What steps into their place is not easily understood as a martial art. It is stillness.

≈

During my late twenties, I lived in a city in the southwestern desert. There was a college nearby, and I enjoyed walking my dog on campus in the late evening. That evening, it was cool, a rare thing in a place where the night heat usually swells against your windows and hugs your body uncomfortably. I lived on Central Avenue, the main road in the most urban part of town. In contrast to the neon lights that buzzed and the strip joints that bellowed bass music and smoke every time a patron entered, the college campus was quiet. It seemed safe. Nightly, I walked my dog through the brouhaha of the city to the college campus, where the noise fell away. My dog and I usually strolled to a duck pond where she, an Australian shepherd, gently herded the ducks back into the water if they strayed too far onto land. Infrequently, I saw a few students carrying books on their way home from the library. Otherwise, I was completely alone.

That evening, the sun had set, and the adobe buildings, with their soft curves and tan color, took on an almost human quality. In the unusually cool air, everything seemed forgiving. So I was unprepared for what happened next.

On my way back from the pond, I walked through a corridor, and my dog ran ahead of me. I was a bit worried for her as she ran because she had just been spayed and her stitches still held the skin of her stomach together. The shadows of the pillars in the corridor crossed the concrete in front of me like a maze, and I watched my dog run—and I watched, as if in slow motion, a large, black boot shoot out sharply from one of the shadows and land a violent kick squarely on my dog's abdomen. My dog yelped. The kick lifted her a few feet off the ground. She curled into a ball.

"What the fuck are you doing?" I yelled.

In seconds, I was face to face with a young man, well built, about twenty. His head was shaved. He wore Lee jeans tucked into knee-high Doc Marten boots; he wore a white T-shirt and suspenders. His five friends were dressed identically to him. Their forearms were tattooed with black swastikas and crosses.

"What did you say?" he said.

"I said, 'What the fuck are you doing?'"

His eyes lit up. His buddies circled around me, and he delivered a violent and sickening threat. "I'm gonna rape your ass," he said.

I looked directly at him. I did not back away or move. I said, without yelling, "Would that make you feel like a big man? You kicked a helpless dog. Now you're going to rape a woman."

He stared at me. His friends waited. I waited. He was clearly the leader. I gathered in my head every technique Sifu Liu ever taught me, and every technique I had learned from other instructors since I'd left him. I saw every movement, saw myself executing the movements calmly, without obstruction. The other guys closed in a little. But the leader did not move. I stared at him, and for a split second, I saw him—small, weak, angry, in pain. For a moment, I felt compassion. Suddenly his shoulders sank slightly, almost imperceptibly. But I saw the movement, and I knew what it meant. I took a deep breath, unlocked my eyes from his gaze, and walked through the closing circle of young men to my dog. I checked her stitches. She was fine, so I leashed her and continued on my way home.

As I left, I heard his voice. "I'm going to rape your ass," he called from a distance. His rage echoed through the corridors, but it did not sound like a threat this time; it sounded like a cry of utter pain and powerlessness. I kept walking, tending to my dog.

On my way home, I understood why Sifu had sometimes asked me to stand in one place for an hour. An hour is a long time. It's sixty minutes, or thirty-six hundred seconds. During the five-minute face-off I had with the six young men that night, I could have sworn an hour had passed.

As I walked, I remembered standing in the kwoon. I remembered the pain that set into my legs at about the fifteenth second. If I ignored the pain, it grew stronger. If I recognized it, I became more aware of my legs as *my* legs. After I began to accept the pain, I still had fifty-nine minutes to deal with the thoughts that came into my mind. The first thought was always, "I'm getting out of here." But my legs decided to stay. I stood. It usually took about fifty minutes for my entire life, every mistake I'd ever made, every great achievement I'd attained, to pass before my eyes. Ten minutes remained. My body had quit hurting. I'd quit mulling over everything that made me feel like a piece of crap and everything that made me feel like a god, and then I was left with ten minutes to be exactly who I was. In those ten minutes, my life became *my* life.

After standing like this for several years, you get to the still point more quickly. Eventually it becomes permanently available. I had not sparred regularly for many years at the time I called out to protect my dog. But the stillness became available to me immediately. As I confronted that guy, I was aware that my legs were my legs, my body was my body, my life was my life, and I did not intend to give any part of them away. As I look back, it sometimes baffles me that I remained calm, because I cannot live in that still place at all times, and I cannot test it in daily sparring matches as I did when I was younger. But I trust it remains. I trust it is available, always, to anyone who seeks it. It is innate, I think, in all beings.

Watch wild animals sometime. Their movements will mesmerize you until, finally, you spot an animal that is perfectly still. In that moment you will see that it is not their graceful, powerful action that allows them to survive; it is their stillness. Once they become tangled in a fight, a certain amount of damage is already done. If the animal is predator or prey, it relies on absolute stillness until the last possible second.

Though Sifu never told me the reason behind the standing practice, I eventually understood. Standing in one place was what I was doing in every sparring match I'd ever entered. Movement went on around me, furiously at times, and I remained at the eye of the storm, an observer able to slow things down, to understand.

Maybe it wasn't qi that was so important after all. Maybe it was just being there, practicing, listening, and eventually sparring. Because sparring is a little bit like a condensed can of life. Things come at you. You can defend against them, absorb them, watch them from a distance, step into the middle of them—or you can pick your path and stay on it, regardless of what falls in your way. If you react to every obstruction, you'll never have time to act.

Watch a wild animal. It will never act in any way that betrays itself or diminishes its own power. It will never give way to any motion that is less than perfect, and its every action will begin with stillness.

EMBRACE TIGER,
RETURN TO MOUNTAIN

Looking back, it seems strange that a man who was fifty years my senior and spoke a language half a world away from anything I understood could enter my life and, though distant from his own native land, could bring me home; but it is what happened.

I was eleven years old. In the past two years, my military family and I had moved from Colorado to Illinois to California. Now we were moving from our current abode to a house three doors down. That morning, I lay in bed too long, considering the task at hand. It would not take a moving truck. We would carry our things in wheelbarrows and wagons. We would take our couch out of the house and, like ants carrying a rubber tree, we'd parade that couch down the sidewalk and up the stairs of the new house, which would wait for us with screen door propped open, neighborhood kids running in and out, neighborhood adults watching us, sometimes helping us, the whole wide world, it seemed, checking out the innards of my new bedroom, our new home sweet home, all for a twenty-five-dollar cut in rent.

In school, I was tremendously shy and contemplative; but at home, I was often the one they turned to in order to get things done, even though I was the youngest of four. I would have to get up cheerfully, go out there, and get that couch moved down the street. I would laugh while I was doing it, make jokes.

The neighbors showed a great interest in our work. "Moving three doors down, huh?" a man called from his porch. "Yep," I called back. He and his family stood in their doorway, watching.

By twilight, we were all moved in, and I was back on my bed, resting in the relative calm, watching the rose- and peach-colored clouds reflect off the bare white walls. It was a markedly cool evening in Los Angeles, and there was something about the cool air that made me feel the way I'd felt in Colorado when I came in from playing hide-and-seek in the late evening. My skin carried the musty scent of grasses, and I felt tired to the point of peacefulness. Maybe that's why I went out walking.

Our little close-in suburb of L.A. was mostly concrete, so I walked down alleys lined with trash cans and old sofas, cut through backyards lush with green trees that were plump with oranges glowing in the evening dusk. As I stepped from one yard into an alley, I saw the light of a garage casting out onto the blacktop. I had seen this before—usually a guy working on his car or a kid sitting in a lawn chair smoking a cigarette. As I approached the doorway, though, I turned. Under the weak, grainy light of one light bulb, there was a man. His body was lithe. He was, I assumed, about sixty years old, and he was dancing, alone. He wore a uniform that looked frightening to me, like something from a prison—matching grey jacket and pants, both loose as pajamas. The way he moved, however, did not frighten me. It calmed me. I thought at first he was a ballet dancer, the way he leapt into the air. His hand movements were nothing like ballet, though. It almost looked as if he was fighting, but his hands remained open and soft. He never threw a punch. He never showed any anger. He moved like a gymnast performing a beautifully choreographed floor exercise. He had that kind of animal certainty and strength.

I realized that I had seen the man before. There was a park nearby, a postage-stamp-sized piece of green smack-dab in the middle of the endless blacktop. A few trees sprouted from the center of the green, and though it was nothing like the wilderness in my Colorado home, it was redolent of that wilderness. For that reason, I loved the patch of grass, the few trees. It had become, to me, a kind of solace.

Frequently, when I went to the park, I saw a man there who stood in one position, his arms in half circles as if holding a beach ball. He never moved. I believed he was crazy. Though it was difficult for me to link that stillness to this fluidity, it struck me now that this man, with all his fluid power and grace, was one and the same as the crazy man in the park.

As he danced, time moved more quickly around me, but slower within me. By the time he returned to the center of the garage floor, placed his hands on his sides, and bowed, it was pitch-dark. He walked to close the garage door (his body graceful even then), and tugged the thick rope. During the few seconds before the door dropped closed, I looked at him hard. He had a round head, high fleshy cheekbones, and close-cropped grey-and-black hair. His eyes, though foreign, appealed to me. They did not look particularly kind. They did not look mean. One of them was smaller than the other, and it looked at the world head-on, like some kind of warrior. The other one was puffy, as if he had a cold, or maybe had been crying. That asymmetry gave his face a sense of longing. In that longing, he was not foreign to me.

≈

My family was like any other conservative family in the late sixties, early seventies: opposed to Tom and Dick Smothers, in favor of decoupage, and thrilled with the miracle that resulted from denial. I remember one night standing in the kitchen baking cookies with my mother when we heard some atrocious yelling, voices vaguely familiar but more high-pitched than we were used to. As if the little doorway between our kitchen and our living room were suddenly the threshold of a saloon in the

Old West, my brother and father came barreling through. I saw my brother's back first, hunched as if his chest had caved in completely. His body (which seemed strangely like an object to me now) slammed up against the washing machine (also in the kitchen), and I saw the metal fold. Only then did I notice that my father's body was attached to my brother's. For a moment they lay like a heap of laundry on the floor. Then, writhing and grunting, they made their way to a standing position, and fists began flying, nothing I could separate out. I remember only the disturbing sound of fist on flesh. It made the body seem hollow, a resonant, clapping *thud*. I think I recall the exact sound of splitting flesh, and then the sudden stripe of blood that appeared on the orange-and-gold linoleum floor.

I had seen my mother respond to incidents like this before. Courageously, she put herself between the two of them and yelled my father's name in a voice that, even in memory, makes my gut turn to a fist. I stood there, scared, thinking, *I have to learn to fight.* Self-defense did not occur to me. I wanted to be able to protect my mother. My father never hit her, but it felt possible to me. If I had to step in the middle of a fight, I wanted to be more effective than she had been. I wanted to be unshakably strong.

That night at the dinner table, every one of us was particularly polite to one another. No conversation, just lots of pleases and thank yous, while the dent in the washing machine grinned at us from behind the table. When, the next day, my father heard me on the phone telling the story of the fight to a friend of mine, he grabbed the receiver from my hand. "What are you talking about?"

"Nothing," I said.

"You don't go telling such stories about me and your brother. We get along just fine." He held the receiver in front of my face. "Say good-bye," he said. He clicked the receiver down before I had a chance to say anything. It was a running joke I had with my friend Karen. We had never conducted a phone conversation without my dad hanging up on her.

Though I laughed at my father's behavior, it also made me sad. In the evenings or late afternoons, I walked to the garage where I had seen the man dancing. Most of the time I found the garage door closed. But occasionally he was there. I sat in a narrow crevice between two trash cans. I watched him. Sometimes he was working at a table. Other times he was dancing. I had come to depend upon him and his calm presence.

≈

During the summer, I spent a lot of time at Karen's house. Although she and I did not have that much in common (she was in seventh grade and already heavily into drugs), I put myself in her life constantly because her two brothers had set up a makeshift boxing ring in their backyard. For a month or so, I watched match after match. The boys fought with their shirts off, and along the sides of their backs long striations of muscle swelled into hopeful wings as they punched. Though boxing had always scared me, the more I watched, the more I knew it was something I had to do. I had to get in the ring and fight. If I backed away from it now, I knew I would back away forever. Finally, in midsummer, when one guy stepped out of the ring and the girls along the sidelines swooned, I stepped up. "I want to try it," I said.

The guys laughed. "You're a girl," they said.

I stood with my hands out, begging for the gloves. A boy slapped the red vinyl things into my palms. "Go ahead," he said. He rolled his eyes, and the other kids laughed.

I pushed my fists into the soft, padded cotton and pulled the laces tight with my teeth. I stepped into the ring. A kid on the sidelines struck a kitchen pot with a wooden spoon, and the match began.

It was as scary as I thought it would be. I had never been hit in the face before. Fists came flying at me, and I heard my own body, hollow like my brother's and my father's. I felt the tremendous force a punch carries. It was not like in the movies, where two guys stood and whaled on each other for five minutes, each of them suffering only a little turn of the head with each punch. These punches whooshed through my ears and vibrated throughout my body. With one strong blow to my head, the kid knocked me down. I felt woozy. The world went black for a moment.

"Come on, girl, get out of the ring," I heard someone yell.

The voice made me feel so weak, so defeated. I stood up, put my gloves in front of my face, hunched my shoulders inward, and dared the boy to come back at me. Lackadaisically, cocky, the boy started swinging again. A few minutes later, he was on the ground. If he had landed a punch in the last bout, I didn't feel it. I stood over him, my heart pounding. I was not elated or proud. I hated the fact that I had to learn to fight.

He lay face down for a long time; then he turned over. "You're gonna be sorry," he said. He raised his gloved fists at me. "These hands are registered with the police as deadly weapons."

I laughed along with the other kids.

"They are—you can come to class and watch," he said.

"What class?" I said.

We unlaced our gloves and the boy, on the verge of tears, hopped on his bicycle. I grabbed another kid's bike and followed the boy. He rode fast and squealed to a stop in front of the garage where I had seen the dancing man. He pointed. "There," he said.

≈

This was a time before David Carradine became Kwai Chang Caine, before Bruce Lee released his movies in America. Few people had heard of martial arts. Some people knew of judo as a sport. It was mostly something practiced by the police and Japanese athletes. That's the way I understood it. I had heard of a mystical, killing art called karate, and I knew that a "black belt" was someone so highly trained that he did, indeed, have to register his hands with the police (a complete myth, of course).

I believed the black belt had superhuman powers. It was not the *way* he punched or fought that made his hands deadly, but rather some kind of dark power that informed his body. His hands were like poison-tipped darts, I assumed. One touch, and you could be dead.

≋

I sat with my back against a cold, concrete wall, but that was not the reason I was shivering. I was *in* the garage now, not pinched between two trash cans, wishing. I was in plain sight of the man who was dancing in front of half a dozen or so young men who tried to follow along. I don't know what it was about the way he moved; I could feel it in my body, like a small echo, some sound or gesture I remembered, though I had never seen it before. When he moved, it felt like my body moved with his. The way he danced caused me to shake as if it were twenty below zero, all that action going on inside me when I had to sit still.

When the group of students had completed their dance, the Chinese man paired the guys up and then walked directly to me. He offered his hand in greeting. "Liu Chih-Xiung, Sifu," he said with a thick accent. I did not take the chance of repeating his entire name wrong. The boy who had brought me there had told me to call "the old man" Sifu, the proper Chinese name for "teacher", so I settled on that. "Pleased to meet you, Sifu," I said.

It could have been my imagination, a result of so many years of believing that "black belts" had poison-tipped fingers; but as my hand touched Sifu's, it seemed a type of electrical current surged through my body. It felt as if he were bolted to the earth. By now, it was difficult to hide my shaking.

"You try?" he said.

I stood up. Sifu called a student to his side, and then, in a meticulous manner that calmed my shaking body, he showed me what to do, how to move. He stopped at logical junctures and said, "See?"

I nodded.

At the end of his series of movements, the student fell to the ground. "See?" he said again.

I smiled.

"Now you try."

I stepped in toward the other student. Periodically, Sifu touched my hand or my leg with the tip of his finger to nudge me into the right position. He was shy, gentle, and deeply reserved. I had never met a man like that. As Sifu instructed me, and my opponent's body responded to what I was doing, I felt a sort of fulcrum being created. At one point a balance of power shifted, and I knew I had control of my opponent's body. From then on, the maneuver took little effort on my part. "Push down," Sifu said. I pushed, and the guy I was working with landed face first on the mat.

In that moment I felt an ocean of possibility sweep through my body. If I learned this, if I could just learn it, my life would change. The fear would go away. The anger might subside. Now, however, the shaking resumed. There was nothing I wanted more.

"Is that karate?" I said.

Sifu shook his head no. "Nan Quan Shao-Lin boxing. No karate." Without further discussion, he gestured for me to sit down.

I was disappointed. I *had* to learn more. I sat down, but as the man walked away, his thin body so graceful and strong, I stood up again. "Sifu!" I said. He turned. "May I come back again?"

He nodded. "You may come back," he said.

That night, when I went home, I felt, already, a stronger sense of who I was. I had a nugget of something that could not be taken from me. I could become strong and formidable in the most physical, real, inexplicable way.

≈

The classes were disappointing at first. I attended for a month before Sifu even approached me. When he finally did, he took me aside and taught me a few moves: stances, hand positions for striking, front kick, back kick. He didn't speak much, and when he did, I didn't understand him. I worked out virtually alone in the back of the kwoon, trying my best to learn the necessary forms.

Forms (*kuen* in Chinese) are vaguely akin to shadow boxing. They are choreographed routines a martial artist practices on her own in order to learn to move with the grace and power essential to all martial arts. They are like scales when a person is learning music. You are supposed to practice them until your body moves that way fluidly, without memorization or thought. Then, in the event that you are ever attacked (or in a sparring match), your body simply responds. The expectation is not only to be good at forms; it is to transcend their choreographed movements. It's like the difference between classical music and jazz; in one, you read the notes on the page and play them, more or less, the same way every time. In the latter, you read the notes on the page in order to free yourself from them.

The forms in Shao-Lin boxing are thought to be derived from a combination of historical sources, one of which is the animal dances performed by the ancient shamans of China (hence, martial arts' association with healing). Each form, to one extent or another, imitates the way a wild animal might defend itself when attacked. The monks and nuns of the Shao-Lin order who created gong fu (synonymous with Shao-Lin boxing) learned about self-defense through watching smaller animals defend themselves against larger animals in the wild. When I was a kid growing up in L.A., missing the wilderness of my home in Colorado, the gong fu animal forms (as they were called) satiated some very deep need in me.

As I worked out in the back of the kwoon, however, I knew I was not very good at the animal forms. My kicks and hand strikes were sometimes fast, less frequently graceful. Ultimately, though, it didn't matter. Even in the awkward, out-of-rhythm, off-kilter way my body moved, I could feel within me the absolute beauty and precision of the form. It was like when you're singing along with Aretha Franklin, and you believe your voice is just like hers, you feel the potential in your heart to sing exactly that way. It did not matter to me that I didn't have the voice yet. I would work hard to get it. The moves made my body feel like song.

It was different than singing though because, here, I felt I had potential. Nobody told me this from the outset. I could just feel it in my body. As I learned any new technique or form, it was as if I was remembering, rather than acquiring.

I knew, also, that something was happening to me. As I attended classes with Sifu, I also kept up boxing. By the end of the third "season" (we broke the matches up into arbitrary seasons), I was declared "the Champ." The boys who had laughed at me for lacing the gloves on the first day now looked up to me. They came to my house and asked me to play with them. They included me in everything, from catching spiders to minibiking. I was not only the champ; I was one of the gang.

≈

Though kids are not supposed to get sore, I nearly needed crutches after each Shao-Lin boxing class. There was a rule that any new student could attend only once a week at first. The notion made me split a gut. It would have been physically impossible to attend any more than once a week. After each class, my muscles felt wrapped in sharp fishing line. When I moved, the wire cinched down, like some kind of torture meant to slowly sever each fiber from the bone.

Maybe half a year in, however, my body stopped hurting. I was less winded than I had been before, and I had developed the strength to follow along with the drills. I could do a hundred push-ups, twenty or so pull-ups, and a half dozen "Shao-Lin tiger push-ups" (a maneuver designed to tweak every muscle in your upper body). What's more, I saw the appearance of my first real-live muscle. At the end of the summer, I had entered junior high. I was undressing for gym class one day, and as I turned my arm inward at the shoulder, the distinct striation popped out.

"Where did you get that?" a girl called out, as if I had just found the coolest item ever at the shopping mall.

I blushed. "I don't know," I said.

She called the other girls around me so I could show them. "Oh my god, how cool," they said.

I said, "Thanks," and I blushed again, telling them it was nothing. Truth was, however, I felt like celebrating. There was, indeed, a muscle just beneath the surface of my skin. It was perfectly shaped, like a long, bulbous fish. I could carry this muscle with me everywhere. I was immediately quite fond of it.

Sometime after that, I and my muscle approached Sifu. "I've been coming here almost six months now," I said. "Is it okay if I come to all the classes?"

He thought for a few uncomfortable minutes. Finally he said, "Yes. It's okay."

≈

I thought the other classes would be even more exciting than the Thursday afternoon "open" classes. They weren't. Often, however, I was the only student who showed up. Still, I came regularly. Though the private instruction was sometimes socially awkward, it was a price I was glad to pay. I was learning the forms faster and in more detail than I ever could have in the group classes.

When I showed up a little late one day, I could see the relief in Sifu's eyes. "You always show up," he said.

"Yes," I said.

He explained to me that "too many people started out with the head of a tiger and ended up with the tail of a snake." Their interest fizzled out.

My interest did not fizzle, but at the same time I could see why the other students might have been a little uninterested. What he taught in the intermediate and senior classes looked nothing like what we learned on Thursdays. I was even beginning to doubt that what he was teaching there was martial arts. It involved a lot of standing in one place and breathing deeply into the lower *dan tien* (an area a few inches below the navel where, according to Chinese medicine, qi is stored). One day, I arrived early and rolled out the mat, as usual. When the door from the house to the garage opened, Sifu stood in the threshold, his finger wagging back and forth. "Ah-ah," he said. "No mat."

"Huh?" I said, confused.

"No mat, no hitting the bag, no workout for many months," he said. Sifu assumed a low horse stance, his feet two shoulder widths apart, knees bent so that his thighs were parallel to the ground. He placed his arms in half circles in front of him and began very slowly rotating his hands, palms facing in, then palms out. I knew, by now, this was his way of teaching—no words, just illustration. I followed his action. When, a few minutes later, he straightened his legs to stand, I followed his lead.

"Ah-ah," he said, finger wagging again. I knew what to do. I resumed the strenuous stance. Sifu circled me, occasionally reaching out to correct the angle of my hands or tapping my toe to turn my foot inward. When he was satisfied with my stance he left the kwoon.

When you're holding a position like this, thoughts scream through your mind, trying to drown out the discomfort. *Where were the other students? Why couldn't I hit the bag? Why no mat? Why did he leave the kwoon? What was he doing right now, reading the morning paper? What kind of idiot was I to stand there, waiting, just because some old man came out and asked me to stand there? No, he didn't even ask me to do it, he just did it, and I followed his action, like a sheep, and now there I was standing like an idiot in a grungy, stinky garage, and why, and for what, and shit, my legs hurt.*

When Sifu finally returned, my first impulse was to scream at him, "Where did you go? How rude!" Then he began doing a kuen. My eyes rested on his beautiful movements. When he was done with the form, he tapped my shoulder. "Good," he said.

I stood upright, shook out my legs.

"That's all today," he said.

"Excuse me?"

He smiled broadly. "I'm going to market. Will you join me?"

The question caught me off guard, but I didn't think twice. I knew he was planning on teaching me some esoteric, Chinese market gong fu lesson. I called my mom to ask permission, and then Sifu and I hopped on the crosstown bus.

When I entered the market I felt as if I had stepped into another world. In the meat department, an entire pig hung from a metal hook. The animal's empty eye sockets looked eerily human. The cans and plastic wrappers were done up in bright colors, shocking pink and sunny yellow. The labels were in Chinese, Japanese, and Korean, and the people in the place did not speak English. Surely this was the place Sifu would reveal to me the black belt's knowledge of the poison-tipped fingers.

In fact, he did nothing but shop. He strolled up and down the aisles, stopping to talk to almost everyone he saw. On that first venture into Sifu's world, I watched this stoic, reticent man become a clown, a gossip, the village storyteller. Talking to his Chinese friends, he gesticulated wildly, his hands moving like the blades of a helicopter, his voice booming, and eyes glittering with laughter and glee—nothing like the intense seriousness he showed while teaching martial arts. Frequently, he snagged me by the arm to introduce me, and for a few sentences he spoke in English. "She is top student," he said. "Very good."

Though his words made no sense to me (I was his top student? Why hadn't he told *me* that?), I could hear his genuine pride. The other Chinese men and women smiled and cooed and very literally pinched my cheeks.

Though it was difficult to accept, I came to believe that this was my mystical, Chinese market lesson—that Sifu, in his own language, was quite the extrovert. He did not speak in short, choppy sentences but instead stood in the grocery aisles with Lee-fong and Yuen-woo and Mei-mei, going on and on so that I almost began to feel bored with him, as I did with my own parents.

Each private lesson continued like this. Along with some teaching about the standing meditation (*zhan zhuang*) I had seen him doing in the park, or about breathing in order to develop qi, I gradually became Sifu's friend. I respected him deeply.

Following his instructions, I did not punch the bag for four months, even in the Thursday classes. He told me not to use my muscles, except when necessary—certainly not to strain them or push them to any limits. Although speed was my greatest asset and the most impressive part of my forms, Sifu did not allow me to perform any kuen at full speed. He slowed everything down, and in that slow movement, the physics of the body became more evident. What the arm did was related to how the foot was angled, and how the waist turned. After a few months, I could not move my hands without feeling it in the soles of my feet.

I know now that what he was teaching me falls under the category of "internal" martial arts (he referred to it as "nei gong," or simply "internal work"). Today, internal arts—those that rely mainly on the cultivation of qi (qigong and taiji, for example)—and external arts—those that rely on muscle power, as opposed to qi—are frequently separated out from one another in practice. Sifu, however, saw them as several integrated parts of a whole. Although I think Sifu had begun inviting me to the store with him simply because he wanted the company, the shopping trips, indirectly, helped me understand what he was teaching. They opened my eyes to another culture, and that allowed me to remain clear and open-minded enough to understand the nonverbal, nonrational lessons he was offering me about qi.

≈

Sifu did not believe in the colored-belt (or sash) ranking system adopted by most contemporary dojos and kwoons. He "ranked" his students only in terms of the length of time they had been studying with him, and since I had been present for over a year now, I was no longer a beginner. I was allowed to spar.

In Sifu's kwoon, there were no gloves allowed in sparring. The hand positions for striking were too varied, and he had taught us how to control our movements so that we could fight full speed, full power, with light, medium, or full contact. He had frequently said the goal of Shao-Lin boxing was to teach a student "This is my arm, this is my leg." If you challenged him and told him you already knew that your arms and legs were your own, he would do a section of a form and ask you to follow him. When you failed, he would say, "If you know 'This is my arm, this is my leg,' why, when I ask you to move like *this*"—he performed his graceful movement—"do you move like *that*," and he would imitate your clumsiness. If you failed to know "This is my arm, this is my leg" in a sparring match, the result was a missed block or a solid, full-power strike. Either way your error trained you to be more aware next time. There was no padded protection to fall back on.

The first time I fought in Sifu's kwoon I discovered exactly how different gong fu was from regular boxing. Although it was more strenuous, it was also more fluid. At least, that's the way it felt in my body. When Sifu dropped his hand (the signal to begin) and danced backward to let us spar, my partner and I engaged in the "fight"; but it felt nothing like a fight to me. There is no other way to describe this: I felt like a river, like wilderness itself. There was no decision to make. Every action just was. With hands flying and feet coming at me from all directions, I felt an utter calm.

When the match was over and Sifu stepped to our sides to indicate the winner, I was ready to sit down. I had taken a number of solid hits, and my lungs were aching for air. "Bow to each other," Sifu said. "Bow to me." He raised his hand above my head, signaling that I had won the match.

Though it felt good to win, something transcended the victory. As those movements streamed through my body so fluidly, I felt strong. If things were sometimes bad at school, if I was too often the new kid on the block, if my father seemed to have a quiet disdain for me, it made no difference. I could do this. I was good at this. It was a tangible, physical thing. I had excelled. Without knowing it, I had turned my body into a pleasingly habitable place. Even for a twenty-five-dollar cut in rent, I did not want to live anyplace else. Those movements and the way they informed my body at that age were, for me, my home. With a certainty I had longed for throughout my entire, little life, I gathered my things, laced my shoes, waved to my friend Sifu, and walked out the door. On the way home, I felt amazed. Somehow, I had found the right place for me on this planet.

Shao-Lin boxing did not take time away from my other interests—writing, reading, painting, drawing; instead, my interests were enhanced by gong fu. I sat at the kitchen table sometimes until two or three A.M. reading a novel or working on an art project. As I sat one night, nearly finished with a detailed pen-and-ink drawing, the light flipped on in the living room, and then my father, clad in a blue terry-cloth robe, appeared in the kitchen. He poured himself a glass of milk and, as he drank it, he accidentally bumped the table. Black ink spilled and poured over my drawing. He looked down at me. Beneath the spill was a week's worth of work.

He had, sometimes, a way of speaking like a baby. When he was not yelling, he was talking to me in this voice, the three-year-old-child voice—punctuated, high-pitched, sad. When he knocked the table, it was this voice he used on me. "Oh, what happened?" he said. "You had such a nice drawing."

I believe to this day that he believed he did not bump the table. The physical sensation of hitting the corner of something as hard as Formica could not break through his denial.

I sat there, staring at my work, and when the living room light turned out again, I tightened the lid on the India ink, washed my pen, and went outside. I meant just to sit on the lawn, staring up at the starless, grey-orange, L.A. sky. Without thinking, though, I started walking. I ended up at Sifu's house. If I had ever possessed a sense of propriety, I lost it in that moment. His porch light was glowing. His low-slung, paint-chipped, wooden house was dark. His sidewalk was the color of honey under the golden street lamp. I walked up to the door and rang the bell.

Within seconds, the lights came on. I heard a clamor, and

his daughter, thirty or forty years old, in big curlers and a bath-robe, opened the door. I did not know what to say. I did not know if she spoke English. As soon as I opened my mouth to speak, I saw Sifu's hand push his daughter away from the door. When he saw me there, he started yelling. I don't know what he said, but in between the beat of Chinese words I heard, "Go, go!" and his hands pushed outward. The door slammed. The lights went out.

I realized I had crossed a line, that I had allowed Sifu to mean too much to me. I had come to depend on him, maybe to love him.

As I walked away, I considered not going back—not to Sifu's kwoon, not to my home. I pictured myself walking to the nearby highway, sticking out my thumb, and joining the throngs of hippies lining America's highways back then. It was a lifestyle that had always appealed to me.

The notion didn't stay with me long. I felt too immobilized, like a deer caught in headlights. Except the headlights kept appearing over and over. Just when I thought I was off the main drag, safely ensconced in the woods, another car appeared, and there I stood, dumb, immobile, staring at the thing that was bound to hit me unless I moved.

I walked into my house, closed the door as quietly as I could, and fell asleep until late morning.

A week went by before I could bring myself to attend classes again. I was embarrassed, and I knew I had irreparably damaged my relationship with Sifu. He would not allow me to come back again. At the same time, I knew Shao-Lin boxing had become something I could not give up, not, at least, without a fight.

When I arrived during my private-lesson time, Sifu was dressed as I had never seen him dress for class before. His attire was strictly Republic of China: navy blue canvas tennis shoes with gum soles (the kind you buy at Kmart for two bucks); polyester slacks pulled up too high over his lower belly; white shirt tucked in, buttoned neatly to the top; white tank-style T-shirt showing through. He was not ready to work out. He was standing above a low table, his body swaying back and forth, as if waltzing slowly. I walked up behind him. "Sifu?" I said, almost whispering.

He did not turn around. I took a few steps closer and looked over his shoulder. He was painting Chinese calligraphy. Without saying a word, he picked up a block of ink engraved with gold Chinese characters and ground it on a piece of wet slate. He shoved a brush in my direction and pointed with his head toward the paper. He painted a perfect circle, a beautiful black openness on white. His demonstration was my cue to follow what he was doing.

My heart surged. He was forgiving me. I took the brush and I painted the circle.

He shook his head, "*Bu dui*, that's wrong," he said, then folded his palm over my hand on the paintbrush. Together, we dipped the bristles into the ink and pressed hard on the paper. I followed what he did, felt the smoothness in his painting strokes; but I was so tired of not communicating. I said, "You know, it would be easier if you'd just explain to me what to do, instead of doing it for me."

Immediately, I regretted my words. They had come out involuntarily, like my walk to his house a week earlier. Sifu stopped my hand abruptly, even forcefully. "Do you know how to speak Chinese?" he said.

"No!" I said, as if he had asked a stupid question.

"I am trying to learn English," he said. "I am learning very well, but after many years, it is not well enough."

Those few words melted an inch-thick layer of anger. I was sitting close enough to him that our shoulders were touching, and his smell permeated my nostrils. It was a combination of oolong tea, old cotton clothes, and sweat. It smelled good to me. He stared blankly at me with his asymmetrical eyes. We had always been swimming across oceans of words to get to each other.

It had never occurred to me that half the communication problem was mine. Though I had learned Chinese words here and there, even a few full sentences , I had never tried to speak them to Sifu. I felt he would judge me; I would make a mistake and be laughed at. In that moment I saw that every time Sifu spoke, he, too, must have been afraid—although it was difficult for me to imagine Sifu being fearful of anything.

After a while, Sifu turned from me calmly and went back to his work.

"I'm sorry," I said finally.

Sifu did not look up. "Don't think about it," he said in Chinese. He pointed to the calligraphy brush he had given me. I picked it up and began painting.

When I went home that afternoon, my father was asleep in his chair, the Sunday paper blanketing most of his body. I sat on the sofa as he slept, his snoring rumbling around the room like his own private thunderstorm. It usually irritated me, the noise. But that day I sat there, trying to recall when I had ever seen my father experiencing the type of joy I felt when I worked out. I had heard tales from my mother, had seen his high school yearbook. Back then, he had a body like Frank Sinatra's and a smile to match. He wore the stylish, pleated pants of the era, and in most photos he was sporting a rakish hat cocked to one side. He had been voted "Best Dancer" by his senior-year classmates. There were black-and-white shots of his body in motion, his arms spread out to catch his partner, a look of exhilaration and glee on his face I had never seen. That day, however, I believed all this joy was still in him somewhere, and that I just could not see it because, somehow, though we were bolted together as a family, it seemed he spoke another language. I kept trying to understand that language, but I came up short. It was undecipherable, distant. I did not feel angry. I felt sad. I felt compassionate. I wanted to crawl inside the words and find out what it was about them that made them so inadequate when it came to families and love.

It's a cruel fate that has been bestowed upon all families from day one, I think: to be dropped into a group of people to whom you are forever bound—but at the same time, you are forever doomed to know them for what they could be. As time goes on, to know them for what they could have been. You rarely see them for what and who they are.

It was as if I was born knowing who my father was, and I had been waiting all along for him to show up. This type of waiting, as the poet Li-Young Lee has said, has "nothing to do with hope," and less to do with patience. "It is simply the way the soul is bent."

Indeed, my soul was bent. I was constantly trying to build a bridge between my father and me, but no matter what material I used, my father would not take the necessary steps to cross that bridge. It was just not in his path. He had other fine points, though, that until that day had eluded me. He was a generous provider. He was, in his own way, loyal. He encouraged me to be my own person and yet, my striving to do exactly that angered him. Time and circumstance had never afforded him that luxury. My mother made up for what he lacked in shows of affection. She loved my siblings and me equally, unconditionally, and with all her might. She opened her heart up to us so much that, sometimes, it collapsed in on itself. It was hard for her to find who she was, something we needed from her as much as she needed it for herself. But a family's love is never perfect. It is, instead, unfailingly complex.

My relationship with Sifu embodied, by default, the beautiful distance necessary for me to conjure my own image of the ideal but impossible family. He had delivered me home, not only to the place in myself to which I would always return, but to the imperfect family to which I would always lovingly return.

≈

When my father announced he was leaving the military and that we, as a family, would return to Colorado, I was elated. Throughout the years I had spent in California, there had been an inchoate tug constantly pulling me back to the place where I was born. We had lived in four houses during our six years in California.

Though I was thrilled, I had no idea how to begin to say good-bye to Sifu. As a military kid, I had developed the charisma to make quick attachments with people, and the coldness to sever them just as quickly. Without notice or explanation, I began cutting gong fu classes regularly. Instead of going to the kwoon, I practiced at home, keeping a record of everything I did to make sure it was up to Sifu's standards. I trained diligently in preparation for the time when I could no longer ask his guidance or turn to him for support.

I made some new friends who lived just down the street— Susie, Mike, Dan. Although I had never been drawn to the California scene of beach parties and cruising the boulevard in a psychedelic van with pot smoke trailing out the window, for a few months it became my passion. During my final month there, I did not visit Sifu once.

On the day we were due to pull out of town, I sat with my face pressed against the back window of our loaded-down Chevy station wagon and waved good-bye to the friends I had just made—Susie, Mike, Dan. I remember to this day thinking to myself, "See, I'm going to get out of town without shedding a tear. I'm ready to go home, can't wait to get there." My mother and father commented on what a strong girl I was.

A few days later, we pulled into a roadside motel at sunset. We had spent the day driving through the desert, where tiny whirlwinds rose up from the barren earth, traveled a few feet, then dissipated, an utter stillness taking over. I don't recall checking into the motel or sleeping that night. But for some reason, I remember walking into the cruddy little bathroom, closing the door, and opening the frosted bathroom window. There was no screen, so the desert was right there, beneath my nose, and the pungent scents of sage and creosote bushes filled my nostrils. I rested my chin on the windowsill and looked out across the land, something beautiful about it to me, desolate and filled with the promise of a richly black night, thick with bright stars. I listened to the whoosh of the cars on the highway and I tried to imagine why those people thought they had to go from one place to the next. I tried to imagine never seeing Sifu again; I couldn't. Somehow, though, I was already hundreds of miles inland. It had already come to pass. I had left without saying good-bye, a weak thing after he had spent so much time teaching me to be strong and resilient. I sat there, too exhausted to cry, my chest heaving with sorrow.

≈

It is thirty-some years after my first lesson with Sifu Liu. After I graduated high school, I returned to study with him for a while. After that, I continued my study steadily with a handful of teachers across the nation. Though gong fu did not become the focus of my life, it is the backdrop of almost everything I do, the home I come back to. To me, it is not something grand or magical (though, like anything, it can seem grand and magical at times). It is not superhuman or mystical. It translates simply as "hard work," and that's what it signifies to me—the day-in, day-out beauty beneath the struggle.

As I do the forms today, I sometimes envision a long wood-plank fence. In it are connected cutouts of every position of the form, and they have been cut there, I imagine, by the thousands of times these movements have been performed, perfectly, by one martial arts master or another beginning some 2,000 years ago. Like early poetry, martial arts have been handed down through history without being written down. Unlike poetry, the language through which they have been communicated is movement; the medium is the body. When I do the form right,

I can feel my body relaxing into this knowledge. The motion becomes effortless—a river moving through rock that becomes a canyon; water sinking into patterns of the earth as my body sinks into history.

By now, this history has become a part of me. I begin and end my days with one of the standing meditations I learned from Sifu Liu. Some mornings, I can feel something is not right. On my own, I readjust, maybe tilting my hands a fraction of an inch inward or outward, and I can feel the palms of Sifu's hands folding over mine to place them in the correct position. From the outside looking in, you would say the adjustment could not possibly have made a difference. It was imperceptible. But as soon as my hands reach this position, memory folds over me. I am home.

Shadows and Light

Jack Blakely, the owner of the Colorado Kung Fu–Karate Center, did not look like a martial artist, certainly not like an eighth-degree black belt who had been studying martial arts since he was three—his father, a black belt in judo. He had a deeply receding, shiny black hairline, which he combed into a curl, like the Gerber baby. His eyes were too small for his face, and his cheeks were pudgy, accentuating his turned-up nose—the kind of nose that takes the upper lip with it, so it looked difficult for Jack to close his mouth all the way. His skin was exceptionally pink—not red, but shiny and pink, and he had a potbelly perched on spindly, though muscular legs. He was not a small man; he was six foot four and bulky. His body did not match his round, baby face, so the overall effect was that Jack looked like a huge, bratty kid. He was all out of proportion. But he was the only martial arts teacher I could find in Colorado who had not given in to the recent commercial martial arts boom.

True enough, Jack's dojo was in a storefront strip mall, but that, I believed, was just a necessary evil: he had to make money. The beliefs he espoused were right on target for my sensibilities. He laughed at the idea of requiring his students to sign contracts. He required no testing fees, and he spoke of colored belts obligatorily, his only concession, he said, to the new popularity of martial arts. Additionally, he had studied with some renowned Asian masters. During his assignment in Vietnam, he had used his leave time to visit other countries, where, once he shared his martial arts knowledge with the masters he met, they shared their most arcane, difficult gong fu forms with him. On the wall were pictures of Jack with his arm around one of two different, smiling Asian men. The men were only about five foot eight, which accentuated Jack's freakish size and proportions. In some photos, Jack and his teacher both held weapons—Chinese sword, saber, three-section staff; in others, they wore white silk Chinese gis and black sashes (the Chinese equivalent of a black belt). Though Jack in a white silk gi looked a little like a Christmas-tree angel, all flowing material with a tiny head propped on top, I was still impressed.

That first night when I came to observe a class before signing up, Jack handed me a piece of paper to fill out. "It's for anyone interested in studying with me," he said. "I run a background check."

I laughed, waiting for the punch line.

He shoved the paper toward me and looked at me sternly, no joke. "It's serious stuff you learn here," he said.

I was only sixteen, unused to this sort of drama. A barrage of emotions ran through me: curiosity, wariness, a little bit of anger, and, mostly, insatiable intrigue. The more he pushed me away, the more I wanted to know what he was hiding. I perused the questions. They asked how old I was, what my license number was, if I'd ever been in a barroom fight or lost my temper at my wife. I filled out the form the best I could.

When the students started filing in for class, they seemed like a nice crew. Except for Jack's wife, they were all men, as usual in martial arts back then, and they had a tremendous respect for Jack; I could tell by the way they greeted him and then got right to work in the dojo. The prospect of continuing my study was looking better and better.

When Jack finally called, "Line up," and the students ran to their places, my heart was pounding with excitement. Then Jack started teaching, and I was certain I had made one of the worst judgments of character possible. Before warming up, meditating, or even performing the traditional group bow, Jack stood in front of the class and broke into an out-and-out rage. His pink face turned bright red, blue veins popping out on his shiny, sweating forehead.

"We are not here to learn 'martial arts.' We are here to learn how to *fuck people up!*" he said. "We're here to teach every goddamned puny-ass bastard who ever looked at us sideways a lesson they will never forget. Let them eat cake now. Four months into your training with me, they will be eating their own god-damned teeth. Mothergoddamnfuckers." He smacked the sand-filled punching bag so hard it folded—a nearly impossible force. "That's their fucking face!" He pointed to the swinging bag. His eyes trembled as he yelled, and when he was not yelling, he was eyeing the students for support.

A few young men in the class were riled up, their adrenaline rushing to their fists. They roared in agreement. Other students looked around at each other, confused. I, myself, was scared. I looked for the closest exit sign, wondering if anyone had run a background check on Jack Blakely. After fifteen minutes of this trash talking, Jack shut up and paced the front of the room like a leopard in a cage, his eyes crazy-fierce, the wall-to-wall dojo mirrors behind him reflecting his eerie image. He no longer looked like the Gerber baby. Finally, he took a deep breath and calmly, methodically, pointed at certain people. "Randy!" he said.

Randy was one of the young men who had been excited by Jack's speech, agreeing with every word. Randy leapt to his feet and ran, front and center. He stood at attention.

Jack walked toward Randy and put his nose on Randy's nose, the stereotype of a drill sergeant. He bared his teeth and whispered, "Get out."

Randy's eyebrows shot up like a puppy dog's. His jaw dropped. "Huh?"

"Get out of this dojo now," Jack said. He enunciated his words. "I'll give you your money back. Just get the hell out. Now!" Randy, confused, waiting for the joke that never came, eventually left the dojo.

Jack pointed to another student and another, until nearly a half dozen young men were asked to leave. By contrast, anyone who had not shown the least bit of interest in Jack's violent outburst was allowed to stay. He explained to the remaining students, calmly, in the voice of a wise old man, "I can't teach people who seek violence. I will not." Then he led the class in a fifteen-minute seated meditation.

That intrigue I'd had when I'd filled out that form was beginning to pay off. Jack Blakely was definitely different from Sifu Liu, but that was not necessarily a bad thing. He was impassioned, unique, perhaps a brilliant teacher. He walked an attractive line between machismo and gentleness. His staged outburst was, I decided, rather effective.

During my first private lesson with Jack (all students had to begin with private lessons), he demonstrated for me his Drunken Monkey form. It was superb—a 264-movement routine (that's a *long* routine) designed to confuse the opponent with seemingly drunken gestures. While doing the form, Jack moved, literally, as you would imagine a drunk monkey might move, with wide, fluid arm movements and "sacrifice techniques," during which he rolled to the floor, then leapt to his feet, sometimes standing on one leg and then falling forward, swaying, kicking, punching. Every movement of the form looked deceptively out of control, when it was, in fact, precise and exact, an earmark of a true drunken form, a moving paradox. To watch Jack's huge body twist and leap in this manner was like watching an old-growth redwood suddenly bend like a willow. It seemed surreal. While he was doing the form, even Jack's face seemed beautiful—calm, focused, serene—and when he was done, I couldn't help myself. I applauded.

As soon as he caught his breath, however, it was as if a different person stood in front of me. He smirked and puffed out his chest. "Pretty cool shit, huh?" he said.

It turned me off. I nodded, being polite.

"Never seen anything like that before, have you?"

I started to say, "Yes, I have seen my former teacher do drunken forms, but I am not very good at them." But I did not get even the first syllable out.

"Yeah, someday I might teach you something like that," he said. "For now, let's teach you a basic front kick."

I had learned from Sifu Liu that when entering the school of another teacher I should not "flaunt" my previous knowledge. "Beginner's mind," Sifu called it. "Never assume you already know what is being taught." So even though the basics for each style are pretty much the same, I was open to learning Jack's way of doing a front kick. When he demonstrated, I looked for any nuance of difference between what he was teaching and what I already knew. The knee came up, pointed at its target; the leg extended as if the knee were a door hinge, then snapped back into "chamber" (the thigh parallel to the floor) before lowering to the ground. There was no difference, so I did the kick I knew how to do.

Jack chuckled. "That's pretty good," he said. He had me repeat the kick a few times, then he moved on to the side kick. He demonstrated. I looked for nuances, then did the side kick I had learned from Sifu Liu. That's when I found out that, maybe, there was a difference between Sifu Liu's philosophy and Jack's.

Jack looked me up and down, his little eyes narrowing, getting lost behind his pudgy cheeks. "Where'd you study before?" he said.

"California. Mostly Southern Shao-Lin. But I'm a total beginner here," I said, adding the last part quickly, respectfully.

He let out a huge laugh. "Damn right you're a beginner here. Southern Shao-Lin Bullshit," he said, as if that were the full title of the style I'd studied. "I hear one word about Southern Shao-Lin Bullshit while you're in my dojo, and you're out. 'Oh, but I did it this way before, Sensei' or 'This form is different than how I learned it before.' I don't want to hear none of that shit. I mean it. I don't even want to hear your pansy-ass teacher's name. I am your teacher, or I am not your teacher."

He paced the floor a bit, for emphasis, then turned to me. "I am the only one. Got it?" he said.

I stood there flabbergasted, waiting for that elusive punch line, for Jack to fess up that this was one of his strategic plays of machismo and ego. I expected the wise man to appear and for Jack to ask me profound questions about my previous study. When that happened, I would make it clear that his martial arts were far superior to mine *and* to Sifu Liu's, as Sifu Liu had instructed me to do under all circumstances (whether I believed it or not). I had it all planned out.

"Got it?" Jack said again, louder.

I waited longer, until it became clear that this was not a show. I had a sick feeling in my stomach. "Yes, sir," I said, though I don't believe I had ever said "Yes, sir" before in my life. But it seemed appropriate, even necessary to my survival in that moment.

Cautiously, Jack began my lesson again, though he used a slightly different approach. He walked behind the Chinese paper screen that separated his desk from the dojo. When he returned, he was rolling his desk chair onto the dojo floor. He plopped down, lit a Lucky Strike, inhaled deeply, and said, "Let's see fifty front kicks, low, middle, high."

I did fifty front kicks aimed at the groin, then the solar plexus, then the head.

"And fifty side snap kicks," he said.

I did fifty side snap kicks, left, then right, and the lesson continued in this manner: rear kicks, then three sets of fifty punches—singles, doubles, and triples—each one followed by a set of fifty sit-ups and twenty-five push-ups.

Jack's smile had not returned. "Most girls do push-ups on their knees," he said.

Remembering what he had said about not carrying anything over from my lessons with Sifu, I dropped to the floor and did twenty-five push-ups on my knees. When I stood up again, he said, "And another twenty-five push-ups."

I did the push-ups, and when I stood up again, Jack laughed. "That's for doing *girls'* push-ups when you're strong enough to do them the *right* way." Then he gave in a little. He looked at me sideways and half-smiled. "You're pretty strong."

"Not really," I said.

He laughed again, this time as if he was happy with my performance. "Okay, lesson's over." He walked out of the dojo and bowed at the door. I went into the bathroom, changed out of my gi, and bowed as I left the dojo. With my head lowered toward the ground, I felt a strong sharp thump on my skull, solid enough to raise a knot. I looked up to see Jack standing there, looking down on me.

"You took your eyes off me."

"We're not supposed to bow when entering and leaving the dojo?" I said.

"Bow, yeah, but look at your opponent, even when you bow."

"You're my opponent?"

"Trust no one!" he said.

≋

There's a certain smell to a dojo or kwoon. It's the sweaty scent of a regular gym mixed with the smells of rubberized mats, wooden staffs, and the metallic scent of swords and sabers. It's distinct and universal, I believe, to every martial arts school in the world. After a while, your gi takes on the scent of the place where you train. There's no getting around it.

As I carried my rolled-up gi to the car that night, the scent of Jack's school was already beginning to permeate the cotton. I wanted to wash the thing immediately. I thought perhaps I'd just had my first and last lesson with Jack Blakely. While his knowledge was vast, I didn't know if I could tolerate his arrogance, and his personality was so slippery: he claimed to abhor violence and then seemed to indulge in the drug a little too much himself. I didn't want to "trust no one," but I wasn't sure if I trusted him. I weighed these thoughts cautiously. Like any teenager, I hated to be wrong. I had chosen Jack as my teacher for very real reasons, and I did not want to go back on them. I rubbed the bump appearing on my head, ducked into my car, tossed my gi in the back seat, and, instantly, my internal monologue turned quiet. Next to the gi I had worn for my first lesson with Jack were the tattered clothes I used to wear when I studied with Sifu. I had brought them in case wearing a gi and white belt to a first lesson looked presumptuous.

I sat in the car and inhaled deeply, noticing the way the smell of something can take you back. Months before we started packing up to move to Colorado, I began downplaying all my relationships in California—my friends, my teachers, and Sifu. By the time I left California, I truly believed Sifu meant little to me. But a few months into my arrival in Colorado, I found that he was not so easily eradicated from my heart. That day in the car, it was as if he were sitting next to me. I could smell his scent, redolent of tea, incense, and sweat, could almost touch his unusually smooth skin. I recalled the first time he taught me a back kick, how I fell flat on my face, literally, and how Sifu stood above me offering no pity yet no judgment. Graciously, he waited for me to try again. He would have waited there, silently, all night. He would not have said a word.

Emotions are like rivers when you're sixteen. They steer their own course and shoot off in tributaries that seem unconnected to their origin, each emotion seeming like the only *real* emotion you have ever felt. I started up the car, tears in my eyes, missing California and Sifu and, at this distance, finally realizing the extraordinary privilege I had been granted when I'd studied with him. When I stopped at the first traffic light, I was limp with sadness and longing. And by the time I hit the second stoplight, I was utterly, outrageously, blatantly pissed off. Jack had not only insulted Sifu, he had insulted me and everything Sifu had taught me. I wanted to fly Sifu in on the next jet plane, set up a sparring match, and watch him easily and methodically kick Jack's ass. I was already planning a way to get the money for the ticket.

And then I thought, *No ticket necessary!* I could do it for him. No, I could not kick Jack Blakely's ass; I would not even get in the same ring with the guy. He was an eighth-degree black belt. He would have picked me up like Godzilla picking up Mighty Mouse and flicked me out the window.

What I could do, however, was go back to Jack's dojo, play by his rules, and calmly, quietly, defeat him at his own game. My parents had already paid the forty-dollar bimonthly fee (a fee they had never paid to Sifu). I decided I would stick it out with Jack for at least that long.

≋

When I showed up for my next lesson, Jack was leaning back in his office chair, his feet propped up on the desk, smoking a cigarette and eating three Big Macs. He smiled when he saw me. I bowed, looking him right in the eye, then entered the dojo. When I came out of the bathroom, Jack had changed from his jeans, T-shirt, and motorcycle boots into his black gi. He placed his left open palm over his right fist and bowed, a Shao-Lin style greeting that illustrated a shield (the palm) covering a weapon (the fist), a traditionally kind gesture. I took it as a sort of peace offering, a sign of mutual respect.

"You're going to learn how to fall today," he said. Though I thought we were alone together in the dojo, I heard the door of the men's bathroom close. I looked up and another man, a brown belt, was standing in the middle of the mat. "This is Dred," Jack said.

I bowed. "Pleased to meet you, Greg."

"Dred," he said.

I had heard right the first time, and I wondered if his parents had tried for Fred but missed a letter, or if Dred had chosen the delightful name for himself. I smiled. "I'm sorry. Dred. Pleased to meet you."

He nodded.

Though I had learned from Sifu Liu how to roll when thrown, I had never learned how to break the fall with my arms, so the whole lesson was new. For the front fall, for instance, Jack told me to jump into the air, flatten out my body in midair, then belly flop onto the mat, bending my arms in front of my body to break the fall. Theoretically, if I slapped the mat hard enough, my hands and arms would absorb most of the shock. I followed his instructions, leapt, and, to my surprise, it worked. I could hit the mat with an impressive splat and feel virtually no shock throughout my body. Even when Jack pulled a chair out and told me to jump off it and land flat, I felt okay about it. The lesson was going well. Then Jack said, "Dred," and Dred, who didn't seem to be the brightest crayon in the box, lumbered over to my side. He stared at me.

"Dred's testing for black belt next week," Jack said. "This'll be good for you and him. He can practice his throws, and you can practice your falls."

For the next twenty minutes, Jack called out reaps and sweeps and shoulder throws and hip throws, and variations on the themes of all of these, and Dred grunted and *kiai*ed and took me down with incredible force, landing, sometimes, with his knee in my rib cage. Surely he was getting about as much practice throwing me, at five foot six and one hundred pounds, as he would have gotten by tossing a wet piece of rice paper around the mat. I was unfamiliar with the throws that Jack was calling out, so I didn't know what kind of fall to expect. (I understand now that this is a lot to ask of a person who has just learned to break a fall.) When Jack called out "leg wheel," I quickly guessed it would be a kind of sweeping, wheel-like motion, and I braced myself for that kind of fall.

Dred, however, grabbed my lapels, twisted me to the right, then stepped in and threw me over his hip. As I was on my way to the mat, he swept his leg back, twisted my whole body to the right, and dropped with me to the mat, making it, in fact, a *dropping* leg wheel. As I learned later, any dropping throw increases the power at least twofold.

I wish I had seen the throw as a spectator would have seen it, for many reasons—the least of which was that I imagined my head must have momentarily flattened as it hit the mat, a truly unusual sight. But I was not watching; I was experiencing, and what I was experiencing was quite like a cartoon image on TV. Everything went black—a different kind of black than night—and bright stars, red, blue, yellow, circled in my own private galaxy. I don't know how long I was down, but when I stood up, Jack said, "Okay. Good lesson."

He bowed to both Dred and me, then left the dojo.

As I changed, I felt okay, but I was a little drowsy, and my spirits were low. I walked out, said good-bye to Jack and Dred, who were sitting at Jack's desk chewing the fat, and I walked to my car. Before I opened the car door, however, I felt so nauseated I had to crouch on all fours to get my balance. I sat there, kneeling in the parking lot for a while, and the nausea went away—or so I thought. During the half-hour drive home, I stopped half a dozen times to pull to the side of the road and empty my gut into the gutter.

When I got home, my mom was waiting for me, as usual. I felt guilty, as if I had been out drinking or something. I knew if she knew what I had been doing, what I had allowed other people to do to me, she would have been furious. If I let on even a little bit, she would not have allowed me to go back, and I was determined not to let Jack get the better of me.

"How was class?" she said as I entered.

"Good," I said. "I'm learning a lot."

She was somewhat skeptical of Jack, and though she voiced her complaints, she always allowed me to make my own judgments. "You sure?" she said.

I nodded. "But I'm tired. I think I'll go to bed early."

My mother kissed me good night, and I walked downstairs to my bedroom.

I lay on the bed, one arm flopped over my eyes. At this time in my life, I had never been drunk, so I had nothing with which to compare the sensation. It scared me. I felt like a piece of lint caught in a whirlpool drain; I kept sinking down and down into more and more spinning, spinning. When I closed my eyes, the room spun around me. When I opened them, the spinning slowed like the Tilt-A-Whirl at an amusement park, but if I left them open very long, the ride started up again, the room spinning fast, no way to stop it. I spent the better portion of that evening hanging over the toilet with five or six towels covering my head, trying to muffle the sound of my retching.

≈

Perhaps it was an I.Q. test. If so, I failed miserably, because, yes, I had a concussion, and yes, I went back for another lesson—my last one before I could join the group classes. This time when I arrived, Jack was already in his gi, and it seemed as if he had been working out, perhaps practicing a form. He was sweaty, out of breath, and in a good mood.

"Loren," he said with a big smile. "Hurry up and get changed. I have some goodies for you this week."

If my body had taken control of me, it would have turned and run, screaming all the way out the door. But my will would not allow it. I nodded, my head throbbing as I tried to imagine what new, boot camp–like test he had for me this time. While I changed from my cords into my gi, I tried to look forward to the lesson, to be optimistic, but every time I felt a little bit positive, a booming voice in my head cried out, *you idiot!*

I squelched the voice, gritted my teeth, and came out of the changing room, looking down as I walked, still adjusting my belt. I took a few steps forward, and I stopped. On the floor in front of me I saw two huge, hairy bare feet. I followed from the ankles up to the knees, up to the face of Dred. He smiled and bowed. My body stiffened with fear. I clenched my jaw, wondering what happens to a person's brain if two concussions hit it within a week, and wondering what had already happened to my brain in general: what the hell did I think I was I doing there?

I turned from Dred and bowed to Jack. "Well," Jack said with an exaggerated drawl. "Tell you what. I know, with your talent, you're going to fly through these belt requirements, Loren."

"No, I'm sure I won't," I said, hoping that humility would satiate the beast.

"So I thought I'd give you a taste of what the upper levels are like."

I felt weak inside. I didn't know if I could take it again, more black-belt techniques practiced on me by the man with that horrendously appropriate name.

"And besides," Jack said, "you owe good old Dred a few bumps and bruises."

I turned quickly toward Jack in disbelief.

"You'll be throwing Dred around today. Is that okay?" he said.

"Yes, yes. Fine," I said.

"Okay then, let's get started. This is from second *kyu*," he said, referring to brown-belt, second degree. Slowly, methodi-cally, he taught me some beautiful moves that, when broken down, became efficient fighting techniques. As Dred came at me with a right punch, I stepped in and sent him flying over my shoulder and crashing onto the mat, flat on his back. As he came at me with an overhand blow, I sidestepped and used his own momentum to send him splatting face first to the ground. It felt good. It was not the same as studying with Sifu, but it felt good. I felt not only graceful and powerful, but confident that I could apply what I had learned. For a woman of my size, that was tantamount to a kind of freedom I had never experi-enced before. Throughout the entire lesson, I kept waiting for Jack to turn the tables on me. It never happened.

≈

While many people believe that martial arts and self-defense are synonymous, they are not. How much "martial" and how much "art" you get depends on your teacher and the style you're learning. If you're learning martial arts with self-defense in mind, it is essential that you select an art designed for your body type and psychological makeup.

Jack surprised me the first day he taught me self-defense. He had a gift for perceiving an individual's physical strengths and weakness and channeling them into very effective tech-niques. His explanations were concise and clear. Although I had seen self-defense practiced at other schools, it had always seemed artificial, even ineffective. The "attacker" and "defender" stood a good distance from one another. I thought, *Who attacks someone from five feet away? A person who is angry or wants to overtake you gets right up on you most of the time. There's often little room to do such a fancy kick.* On one occasion I voiced this concern to the sensei of a very hard system and he replied, "Well, you should never let an attacker get that close to you in the first place." But it's a little hard to walk down a city street keeping a five-foot radius of space around your body at all times.

During my lesson with Jack, he blew apart that approach to self-defense. He taught me to fight extremely close in, based on the simple notion that the most effective part of any weapon is the *end* of it (a knife, chain, fist, whatever). So, against common sense, I learned that the best defense is usually to step *into* your opponent, closing the distance and thus nullifying the effects of the weapon. "Learn to use your hands close in and you have the advantage in any situation," he said. It was a notion I'd embodied in my practice with Sifu, but, perhaps because of our language barrier, it had never been stated so concisely.

I spent that afternoon having lots of fun, tossing Dred around the mat as if *he* were a wet piece of rice paper. When he came at me with a punch, I sidestepped, parried, and helped him along on his journey toward the mat. His size made little difference. Sometimes it even worked to his disadvantage, because more mass has more momentum, and more momentum means hitting the ground harder.

For my final lesson of the day, Jack brought out a knife. He handed it, butt end, to Dred. I was already worn out from our practice, and I looked at Jack with fear.

"You don't want to learn how to defend against a knife?" he said.

"Sure, but . . . you don't have a rubber one?" I said.

"Oh, I'm sorry. You want to learn to defend yourself against a *rubber* knife." He walked to his desk, kicked back in his chair, and crossed his legs. "Here's the defense against a rubber knife," he said. He smirked and lit a Lucky. After a long drag from his cigarette, he crushed it out, then looked at me. "There'd be no reason to defend against a rubber knife, now would there?"

Oh, the arrogance was no longer lying dormant. That snaky man was about to shed another skin. I knew this was it. He had lured me in with his sweet pussycat act, and now he was going to strike. He would have Dred stab me a few times, just to keep me humble. I could not put it past him.

To my surprise, Jack stood up and walked back into the dojo, laughing. "Come on. I'll teach you," he said. "But we don't use rubber knives in this school. We don't use *rubber* anything. With us, you get the real thing or nothing. Right, Dred?"

"Right," Dred mumbled, amused with Jack's witty repartee.

But that was the end of Jack's misbehavior. Both he and Dred took the next fifteen minutes very seriously. Slowly, carefully, Jack taught me how to defend against a knife. "Never look at the weapon," he said. "It'll psych you out. Look at the hand. It's the same as defending against a punch."

When learning a self-defense move, you start practicing very slowly, using no power, no speed, and then you build your way up. By the end of the lesson, I was working at about half speed, half power, defending against Dred's attempted knife attack. The steel blade made all the difference. The precision demanded was exhilarating.

As I walked out of the dojo that day, I felt safe in a way I had never felt before. When I bowed, I looked Jack in the eye, smiled, and said, "Thanks. That was great."

"That's just a taste of what you'll get if you stick around for your black belt," he said.

I smiled. I knew I would stick around.

≈

Over the next few months, I became one of Jack's favorite students. He taught me new techniques before classes started, and he called on me to demonstrate them during class. When a potential new student entered the dojo, he overlooked the guys and showcased my forms and applied self-defense. Dred was still Jack's buddy, but he became a second choice when it came to martial arts. Once, when a man who had studied for years in another system entered the dojo and asked if he could spar with one of Jack's students in order to sample the quality of Jack's teaching, Jack called on me. The potential student stared at me for a minute, took Jack aside, and whispered, "In our school, men do not fight against women."

Jack cocked his head and looked at the guy. He did not whisper. He said, "Well, maybe that's because you're afraid of being beaten by a woman."

I bowed to my opponent. Jack gave the signal to begin, and when, after a five-minute match, I had backed my opponent into a corner and pressed him tightly against a mirror so that he could not defend against anything I threw at him, he called, "How do you get her off you?"

Jack stood in the corner, his arms crossed, laughing uproariously. He laughed for a good long time before he asked me to stop. I stopped sparring, bowed to my opponent, and went back to practicing alone.

Jack was pleased. He looked at the potential student proudly. "You know, most martial arts were created to give the little guy, or in Loren's case, the little gal, an advantage. Size doesn't matter at all. It's spirit."

The man nodded and asked if he could please become Jack's student.

I gobbled up the attention Jack gave me because it came from such an unlikely source. Jack had never planned on liking me. He'd never planned on thinking I was a decent martial artist. He'd believed I would go away in a week. But I remained the only female student who lasted in his school for more than a month or two (with the exception of his wife). He changed some rules for me, such as "No swearing during formal work-outs," and "No dating." (I was asked on a few dates in the beginning.) The problem was, I changed too, although I did not know it at the time.

≋

The thing about fear is, it doesn't go away. Not so with love or pleasure. You say to them, "Stick around, why don't you?" They take off. You may call for them to come back to you, but they're off on new ventures, independent as cats. But fear is loyal. It does not leave. You will do anything to make it go away. It stays. It's the office boy who has a crush on you and thinks of reasons to deliver to your desk. It takes every chance it has to pop in and say hello, as if you missed it.

A class with Jack Blakely was a class in fear. One night he told of the woman in the nearby laundromat who was attacked with a knife and had the guts to grab the blade and break it off, thus saving her own life but maiming her hand. The next night he told the details of the Ted Bundy attacks, the Son of Sam murders. He had inside information. He taught self-defense to police officers and had been on a beat himself. He knew every random attack that took place locally and talked about them at the beginning of every class. He was an endless well of graphic details, like a bad journalist looking for the next gruesome story and horrifying headline.

It was a little motivator, I presume, because fear also abstracts more easily than love or pleasure. You may see someone in love and long to be there with them. You may think wistfully about pleasure as you watch others having a good time, but you can't get there; you cannot feel the pleasure unless it is yours. When you see or even hear something frightening, however, it frightens you. It is not your fear, but it becomes you.

Within a few months of my study with Jack, I quit practicing the forms I had learned from Sifu. My weekends were filled with "endurance training sessions," during which Jack drilled us like boot camp initiates. In his backyard he had constructed an obstacle course. We began the day with push-up competitions, doing hundreds of push-ups until our arms were shaking like the limbs of willows. Same thing with pull-ups, sit-ups, lunges, and squats. We punched the sandbag until our arms would not move anymore. This is not a figure of speech. There was a tickling sensation in my joints, and when I lifted my arms, I was filled with involuntary emotion, as if I would laugh or scream because laughing or screaming was the only "muscle" in my body that had not been wrung dry of energy. My arms were foreign appendages hanging at my sides.

Jack punctuated these sessions by creating violent scenarios and telling us that if we gave in, we had failed. If we gave up here, we would certainly give up when the real situation confronted us. We would die.

Fear. It gets under your skin even when it is not yours.

At one endurance training, a guy did a forward roll to avoid an attack by "dogs" (yes, Jack taught how to defend against animals, too). As he jumped to roll, the man's little toe wedged itself between two bricks and stuck there. It ripped off, clean, the entire toe. The guy tucked for his forward roll, screaming, "My toe, my toe."

Jack walked to the brick wall and saw the toe there, perfectly formed, separated from the foot. It had, apparently, ripped off between muscles, in a manner that caused almost no bleeding. Jack looked at the student. "Well, pick it up and continue," he said.

The student went back to the brick wall, picked up his toe, and carried it and his other nineteen digits through the obstacle course: a ten-foot wall and rope climb; a mud moat (he hopped); tires in a narrow passageway; a "blind alley" where you could be attacked by any member of the class wielding any weapon—but if you misjudged the situation and defended yourself *before* you were attacked, you had to start over again.

The man carried his toe through twice. Then he carried it to the hospital to have it sewn back on.

After five or six weeks of these training sessions, I did not need a five-foot radius of space around me to feel safe when I walked down the street. I created that space psychologically. Nobody got close to me. Everybody was a potential threat. There was no room for error or psychological rest. I was always safe, always on guard—intensely, subconsciously. The fear that shows up nightly on our news report, the fear we read about in tabloids, the fear that entertains us on our movie screens played through my head like a constant reminder of the attention one must pay to the world. I looked at it coldly, fearlessly. I trusted no one.

≈

I made it to my first-degree black belt (sho dan) test in record time, under a year, when others who had been studying for half a decade were still working toward green belt. Though at the outset I would have expected the guys to be resentful of this, they were not. Jack honored me when honor was due, and the other guys, his students, followed his lead.

Normally, the way Jack tested lower-belt students was this: at some point during class, Jack called you out onto the floor. He asked you to do a few techniques, which was not unusual. Then he asked you to do a few more techniques, interspersed with some impromptu self-defense, maybe a form. If you were doing well, he asked the rest of the class to sit down. That's when you knew you were testing. In contrast to today's testing protocol, Jack never tested more than one student at a time, and he never announced a test beforehand. But because the test for first-degree black belt required the presence of two other black belts, and because it spanned a two-day period, Jack notified the student in advance.

I showed up for Saturday class at ten A.M., as usual, and when I walked in, Jack said, "Next weekend, Loren. You're testing for black belt. Saturday and Sunday, all day."

There was a thrumming in my head, and immediately I started rehearsing the moves I would have to perform, from white belt on up, including Jack's whimsical additions—he might ask me to perform any technique he'd taught in any class. In Jack's world, you either knew it all or you knew nothing. And so the rest of the day I was preoccupied, only half into the workout, and it showed. I faded to the back of the dojo. The guys, who usually looked up to me, overlooked me. I was quiet, withdrawn, already concentrating.

Through the haze of my concentration, however, I saw Jack revealing a movie camera and setting it on his desk. Dred and some of the other guys were playing around with it, filming silly scenes and laughing. Jack had some big planks of plywood, larger than the twelve-by-twelve simple pine boards we used to break, a task that was fun to us, rather than serious. ("Boards don't fight back," Jack said, repeating Bruce Lee's famous line.) Out of the corner of my eye, I could see Jack sticking the plywood planks into the gi tops of the guys, then punching them solidly, as if testing them. I tried to ignore the whole thing, reciting in my head all the knowledge I had acquired from Jack.

"All right, let's film," Jack said.

The guys circled around the mat and, obligatorily, I joined them, still lost in my own world. Joey, a green belt, stood on the sidelines, holding the camera. Dred wielded the eight-inch knife blade we used for practicing self-defense. Jack stood across from him, weaponless.

"Ready," Joey yelled. "And action!"

At that, Dred lunged toward Jack with the knife, and Jack, in a few quick movements, disarmed him, took Dred's knife in his own hands, and proceeded to stab Dred in a fast but meticulous pattern, as he had taught us to do when knife fighting. The difference was, he was actually stabbing Dred. At least, that's how it looked. The knife thrusts were real. They did not stop an inch away from the body but instead plunged into the thick board Jack had placed beneath Dred's gi. To the naked eye, it did not look as if Dred was wearing any protective gear.

I was shaken from my reverie. I wanted to scream, "Stop!" but the whole incident took less than a few seconds. Though I knew it was fake, it looked like pure violence. My stomach turned.

"Cut," Joey yelled. "Good!"

Dred, lying on the ground, playing dead, stood up. The guys laughed. "Oh man, that was cool." "Shit, that looked so real." "Goddamn." "Whoowee!"

Jack beamed, his pink face shining with sweat, his narrow-lipped smile forming a tight little half circle on his face.

I tried to gain my composure. I was accepted by the guys by now and did not want to seem different. I said, "Uh, yeah, cool." And I went back to reviewing for my test.

But it happened again. This time another fellow lunged at Jack with a different knife attack, and Jack responded in the same violent manner.

Between one choreographed scene and the next, I stepped

up. I said, "I don't understand. Why do you have to make it look so real?"

"For the camera. We want it to look real on the camera," Dred said, as if I were truly stupid.

"Oh," I said. "What difference does the camera make?"

Jack put on his teaching voice. "You see, I want to preserve on tape all the techniques I have ever taught. I want them to look as real as possible. To show they're effective."

The logic was so flawed I almost burst out laughing. Looking real did not make them any more or less effective. It simply made them look more violent.

For the rest of the day, the guys practiced the graphic knife-fighting techniques, and I found myself a corner of the dojo, where I practiced for my black-belt test. I ignored the filming, plugged my ears against the cheering and the sound of the blade hitting hard into the board. With each solid *knock*, I prayed that the board would hold up, that it would not split at the point of impact.

At midday, their act was raised to a frenzy. They started a new plan whereby, with great seriousness, they pinned packages of ketchup all over the board. When Jack stabbed the ketchup spewed, and the guys acted out their death throes there on the mat. You could not really call it play.

I could have laughed, but it was at that point, I think, that I stopped practicing for my test. I knelt in zazen posture as if to meditate, and the clamor of voices blurred behind the whirring in my head. What was happening in the dojo did seem like a film to me, the sound turned off, the eerie faces of people laughing, cheering about what looked like real violence. By design, the line between reality and imitation was thin as air. As I watched, other memories started up.

When I looked at Jack that day, it was as if I were looking at a double-exposed photo, one ghostly image superimposed on the other. In front of me, Jack narrowed his eyes into pure focus, disarmed his assailant, and "defended" himself by "slitting" the tendons in arms, "stabbing" the body, pressing the blade against the throat. Behind this image, I saw the image of Jack teaching the first night I watched. He stood so calm and confident after his brilliant, provocative speech. "I cannot teach those who seek violence. I will not." He could have turned and walked down an incense-filled hallway; I would have believed he was holy.

The power Jack had over people's image of him was amazing. My first day of endurance training, I had asked Jack about the purple heart medal that hung on his wall with a collection of other military awards.

"Vietnam," he had said. "I was behind enemy lines, and I was shot. But I still carried my buddy to safety. We sat in an anthill for eight hours, waiting for the enemy to pass, and in that eight hours, I bandaged my buddy's wounds, blood gushing from my own gut." He laughed. "By the time we moved out, ants were eating my liver. No shit. The parts of our skin that were not already shot to hell were raw and bleeding. Damn ants eating us alive."

I ran my eyes up and down Jack's body, looking for scars. "Where were you shot?" I said, and one of the guys answered for me: "Spine."

"Yeah, spine," Jack said. "Thought I'd be paralyzed. But I have some artificial discs in there now. Bionic."

I was not a person thrilled with war stories, but I was intrigued with the survival. It seemed Jack had held on to life with such tenacity. For the next few months, I watched Jack closely as he changed from his sport shirt into his gi top. I looked for scars around his spine, for the battle marks on his body. His skin remained smooth, pink, and hairless. I never saw a scar.

These images ran through my mind as I sat in the dojo that day, and in the background I heard Jack saying, "All right, Ricky, your turn. Your turn, Ricky." The knife fighting was still going on. I'd made little headway in my practice for black belt. I took a deep breath and decided I had to get back to it. Though every part of me wanted to leave and never come back, I was not about to give up now. When I stood to resume practice, I saw Ricky standing across from Jack. He was a little guy, quiet, sometimes timid. But now he faced Jack with a knife.

"And, action," Joey said.

There was a flurry of movement, Ricky coming at Jack with an overhand jab, the blade switching from Ricky's hand to Jack's like a feat of sleight-of-hand magic, and then Ricky hit the mat. He rolled around for a while, the bloodlike red stuff pooling around him. Jack and the other guys laughed, and hooted it up. But Ricky kept rolling, curled into a ball.

I was scared. I walked slowly to the mat, my eyes on Ricky the whole way. He was not getting up, and Jack and Dred and the crew were getting ready for the next scene.

Finally, when I was a few steps from him, Ricky stood.

"I'm hurt," he said, and Jack turned, still smiling. Ricky held up his left hand. The blade of the knife ran cleanly through the center of his palm.

"Oh, shit," Jack said. He laughed a little, then walked straight over to Ricky, held Ricky's hand by the wrist, and pulled out the knife. Ricky's knees went weak. Another guy ran to the bathroom and came back with two or three terry-cloth towels. He wrapped them around Ricky's hand. In seconds, they were drenched with blood.

"Loren," Jack said. "Drive Ricky to the emergency room, will you?"

On the way to the hospital my head was still whirring. There was a lump in my throat, a tenseness so strong that my muscles were shaking beneath the skin. I said, "You okay, Ricky?"

He said, "I can't move my fingers."

"You'll be okay, though. You'll be all right, won't you?"

He nodded. It may have been bad timing, but the question was like a pressure around my brain. I thought for a long time before asking. Then I said, "Ricky, you undress with Jack in the men's room all the time, right?"

He nodded, grimacing.

I hesitated. Then I said, "Have you ever seen his scars?" I didn't know if I wanted to hear the answer.

Ricky was rocking back and forth, his hand curled into his chest, his eyes holding back tears. He shook his head.

"I mean, Jack was shot up pretty badly in the war, right?"

"Yeah," he said between clenched teeth. "But he got some kind of plastic surgery or something. You can't see nothing now."

≋

A tendon in Ricky's hand had been severed. When I returned home from the emergency room I lay on my bed, and the double-exposed images continued. But this time, they were of me.

I saw myself with my Sifu Liu, the contemplative, kind, Chinese man who had taught me more about stillness than about movement; it was, he'd said, the heart of martial arts. It was even the heart of self-defense, the ability to remain still. I saw myself doing standing meditation with Sifu in the local park. I saw myself bending my body gracefully, practicing the forms Sifu had taught me, the way my body moved like water, so innocent, so unafraid; I saw Sifu's hand wrapped around mine as he taught me to do calligraphy, the art of writing words that formed like rivers on the page, how those words became my body, a grace and a power that was thought and action combined, the inseparable parts of a whole.

On top of those images, more clearly, as if emerging from a fading background, I saw myself walking down the street, an intense awareness about me, unconsciously pushing people away. I was always on guard now. I was self-sufficient. I was prepared for conflict before there was any hint of conflict, a state of mind Sifu had taught me was wasted energy at best— and dangerous at worst. He believed these types of thoughts would not ward off danger but rather would bring danger closer to me, put me at risk. *Think it, and it happens*—the power of words, the impact of images. Halfway into my study with Jack, I began to see this attitude as a part of Sifu's native culture. I thought, *In China the government controls the press so the people have a false sense of security; they believe nothing bad ever happens.*

By contrast, Jack had convinced me that facing things head-on, looking at the most gruesome events on film or in newspapers, would train me so I could defend myself without emotion. I could be sufficiently numb to violence and at the same time hypervigilant about potential danger.

I lay there on my bed thinking a horrible thought: I was becoming Jack—and I did not even know who Jack was. He espoused nonviolence and then, among his initiates, became so violent that the dojo itself seemed a place of dark worship.

None of us ever said anything about what happened inside those walls, and somehow this made each person feel special, as if privileged by secrecy. We each believed, I think, that the inside knowledge would set us free—free of fear, oppression, timidity, violence.

I tried to recall the first few lessons I'd had with Jack, my impetus for continuing, my intention to prove him wrong. It was a vague memory, shadowed over with desires that had bloomed in me within the recent months: the desire to feel safe; the desire to feel safe; the desire to feel safe.

But there is no feeling so unsafe as watching yourself fade into the background while a new self takes over, one you like less, one who seems stronger, more alien, more aggressive, more set on forcing itself into existence.

For the next week, I practiced like a madwoman. I rose at five A.M. and trained intermittently until evening. I meditated, standing and sitting. I ran for miles, jumped rope, and did push-ups. But during that time I did not do a single technique Jack had taught me. I was submerging myself in what I had known before, the forms and techniques Sifu had taught me, as if by going through the motions I would return to who I knew I was. I felt like I was literally trying to purge something from my body and mind, to return to what I loved: the *art* of martial arts, the art of combining power and grace in a single gesture, of feeling calm and self-confident, of being in complete stillness, the art of the body at peace—with itself, with the mind, with the world. It was from that place and only from that place that I could ever defend myself, if necessary. It was from that place that I would probably not have to defend myself. It was in that stillness that I felt whole.

There seemed no contradiction at all in my mind about learning martial arts and swearing allegiance to nonviolence. When I forgot about what Jack had taught me, I became aware that I was worth defending and respecting, that to ward off violence from myself was nonviolence. But it was not about conjuring fear that did not exist and protecting myself beforehand. It was about being open to what takes place in the moment, expecting nothing, and reveling in the newness of any emotion as it arrives—whether it be love, joy, or fear. That, in the end, is what takes guts. That is what takes self-knowledge. That is what martial arts are all about.

≈

My parents didn't come to watch my black-belt test. My mother said, "I'm sorry. I can't watch all those big guys coming at you so violently. I always want to get up and put myself between you and them. And that wouldn't be good."

"No, that would definitely not be good," I said.

I drove out to the dojo on my own that Saturday morning. I was not particularly excited or nervous. I knew what I knew.

I knew what I had learned from Jack—and some of it had been very good stuff. His forms were exquisite. He really did know his self-defense. But the reason I excelled in his school was, I believe, mostly because of what I had learned before. Jack gave me new physical techniques, but the self-discipline, the self-respect, and the compassion I needed to enact those techniques were in my heart and mind before I came to him, instilled, partially, by my five years of study with Sifu. I had come close to obliterating these values. I had come close to rising to the surface, to believing there was art in something purely martial: the art of war, an abuse of the term, because art brings you closer to yourself, plain and simple. War divides. With Jack, there was a chasm between who he was and who he thought he was. It's one of the greatest tricks of the psyche: what it lacks is what it pulls toward it: the charisma of tyrants, the magnetism of false leadership.

When I walked in, Jack and two men I had seen but did not know well were sitting in three chairs in front of the mirrors. My colleagues, Dred, Joey, Ricky (his hand in a bandage), and the rest lined the walls. They sat in zazen. I can't say this did anything to help me remain calm. I bowed when I entered the dojo, then walked across the mats to the changing room. When I came out, Jack and the two other men stood. Jack said, "Are you ready?"

"I am ready," I said.

"Gentlemen," Jack said. The two black belts on either side of Jack sat down. Jack looked at me. "Bow to me."

I bowed. Part of me respected part of him, and those were the parts of both of us I was trying to hang on to here.

"Bow to your colleagues."

I bowed to the four directions, with great respect for every person there.

"We will begin."

Throughout the first day, I went through every technique and form from the lowest level of orange belt (there were levels of each colored belt) through the highest level of green. At certain points, Jack called on one of the observing students to be what we called "the victim," even though, if you were watching, you would call him the perpetrator. The victim would come at me with different attacks—holds, attempted takedowns, punches, chokes, you name it. I was to defend, and so that I would not get used to defending one size of person or style of fighter, I frequently had to do each technique on two different men.

In between these techniques, Jack would request a certain form, or would request that I spar with a colleague. My sense of how long the first half of the test lasted was impressed upon me by clouds. It was a fall day in Colorado. When I walked into the dojo, the sky was crisp blue, like the inside of a crystal ball. When I walked out, the afternoon clouds gathering over the mountains were a billowing darkness, dense enough so that in the one place where the clouds split to blue sky, striations of sunlight streamed down and lit a bright green patch in the distant mountains that were otherwise grey, streaked with a curtain of rain. The scene was like salve on wounds, the fatigue of my body.

I can't recall anything about the night—if I slept well, if I didn't sleep at all. Everything blurred into the next day, Sunday, when part two began. If I was calm before, I was nervous now, and if I was nervous before, it was for different reasons. The day consisted mostly of weapons defenses: club, chain, knife, gun. It would take every bit of mental focus I had because the guys in Jack's school were trained to come at the person being tested as if it were a real attack. Anything less, and Jack would ask them to leave. They always followed his orders.

The mental clarity that comes with this sort of practice turns the world into a vivid dream. There is a part of you that feels the world moving slowly, sees every movement, feels every sensation with greater intensity. But the part of you that would normally analyze all this is nonexistent. It's probably the only time in a person's life during which they act with absolutely no chance of judging themselves. None. It takes that sort of clarity to succeed.

So it took every bit of mental clarity I had to stand across from Dred as he wielded the same blade I had seen pierce Ricky's hand the week before. The defenses ranged from knife jabs to slashes, to behind-the-neck holds, to the type of showy affair where the assailant tosses the knife back and forth from one hand to the other, the silver blade flashing like a hypnotist's pendulum. I kept hearing Jack's voice, *Don't look at the weapon, look at the arm,* but I kept glimpsing flashes of silver.

I was not yet in the moment, but I knew Dred would lunge nonetheless. Everything was happening quickly, too quickly. We were facing each other on the mat like cats, the silver blade, the silver blade, and then a split second turned to a minute. Dred lunged, and the world slowed, became more vivid, and fell away all at once. There were no black belts sitting in chairs around me, no people sitting in zazen; there was me, standing perfectly still in a park in California, as my first teacher had taught me to do; there was complete silence; there was incredible calm. It lasted what seemed a long time, long enough that I could hear my own heart pounding like a drum inside my chest. A split second later Dred was on the ground and I had the knife in my hand. The first technique was over. I had succeeded. I was now in a state of mind from which I could not be extracted, even with pliers and a good shrink. I was in a different world.

Throughout the rest of the test, I defended against multiple opponents with weapons—knife, club, chain, from three different directions—all at once. The weapons were real, the defenses impromptu. From there, we went to multiple opponents without weapons. Jack started this section off with two attackers, in some ways the most difficult number to fight, and we worked up to ten. Beyond that, it was just arithmetic; what was really being tested was stamina. Fatigue penetrated my body like thousands of needles. That mental presence of mind with which I started had faded to delirium. Either way, there was still no time to judge. But there was a point at which I saw a light at the end of the tunnel. I started to believe I could let up. I started to believe I had made it.

As I did what I knew was my last requirement for the belt, my head started spinning with relief. As if I had known all along why I was there, I recalled the first day, recalled how Jack had wanted to get rid of me. I relived the concussion and my reasons for coming back: to stand up for what I believed in and loved; to confirm that martial arts, heavy on the art, was better than martial arts, heavy on the martial; to make a point about compassion. I had made it. I had succeeded. I had never struggled so hard in my life.

I performed the final movement, and I think I saw Jack smile. I stood in front of him. "Kneel, please," he said.

It was protocol to kneel and face the wall while the judges discussed your performance on a test. I knelt, my body so fatigued it felt the opposite of heavy; it felt so light that I had no control over my muscles, the way a ribbon will flap in the wind no matter how much strength you use to hold it down. My mind was clear, fully present. I heard Jack call my name.

"Stand and face us," Jack said.

I stood and faced the black belts. I knew the next words from Jack's mouth would be, "Congratulations, Loren," and they would be so sweet.

"Steve," he said.

I was confused.

One of the black belts flanking Jack stood up. He and Jack whispered, and then Steve began stretching out. After a few minutes, Jack called Steve to his side. "Bow to me," Jack said.

Steve bowed. My confusion continued. I bowed.

"Bow to each other," Jack said, and it clicked. Though I had sparred throughout my test, though I had defended against multiple opponents for hours, though I had begun at the first belt and worked my way up, Jack was going to make me spar again, this time with a man who was several ranks above me.

"Begin," Jack said.

I lifted my arms into fighting stance. They were ribbons in the wind. I tried to see Steve's openings. He was watertight. We circled, we came at each other, and Jack called, "Point!"

Although Jack did not usually adhere to the popular sparring trend that required two fighters to break between points, he made an exception during tests. I don't know if this was because of the presence of the two other black belts or because he had a modicum of pity on the tester. My guess is the former. When we broke, the point was assigned to Steve.

The contest went on like this until Steve and I were tied, two to two. Three points won the match. If I was moving in slow motion in my mind during the first technique of this test, I was moving in slow motion in my body now. Steve dropped his guard for a second. I let out a tremendous kiai, and I went straight for his solar plexus with all my power. Two seconds later, I was on the floor, my diaphragm fibrillating, the air coming in and out of my lungs like little wings, no breath large enough for me to catch and hold.

Jack stood from his chair, slapped me hard between the

shoulder blades (the antidote for fibrillation). I coughed, and then I breathed again, gulping air as if it were water. I stood.

"Bow to each other," Jack said.

Steve looked at me with sadness and compassion as we bowed.

"Bow to me." We bowed. "Steve, have a seat. Ms. Loren, please kneel."

I knelt and faced the wall. I felt as if I would cry, my chest still heaving, sore from the fibrillation, and my ribs aching from the solid kick Steve had landed. Jack had set me up. I went through the whole test in my head. I had felt good up until that last moment. Some of my forms were the best I had ever done, and the self-defense spoke for itself. I had never before seen Jack throw in that final sparring requirement on any test. My chest was heaving and I was trying to keep everything I felt inside, show no emotion, find the calm I knew was my center. As my breathing began to slow, I heard Jack call my name. Part of me did not want to stand, but I stood. I faced the three black belts, Jack like a tower between the other two men's smaller statures. My head hung low. Jack took one step forward, his face serious as hell. Then he smiled, and he held out his hand to shake mine. "Congratulations, Loren!" he said. "Black belt first degree."

I shook his hand in a daze. I felt like saying, "Really? Really? You're not kidding? What about that one point?" To my surprise, Jack put his arms around me and hugged me—something I had never seen him do to anyone. The other two black belts descended on me immediately. They were genuinely happy, ecstatic. "Best black belt test we've ever seen," one of them said. And again, I felt like saying, "Really? Really?" My vocabulary was zapped to disyllabic sounds of glee and disbelief. "Really? Nuh-uh. Really?"

Steve hugged me so fiercely I thought he would break the rib he'd aimed for with his kick. "I knew you'd run in," he said. "I knew you were tired and you wanted it over with, so I just dropped my guard to lure you in, then put my foot up. You ran right into it."

"I know," I said, rubbing my side.

Then Jack chimed in. "But you know, Steve, she would have had you, normally. She would have had that point. I just wanted to tell you."

I smiled. If I'd learned anything from Jack it was that there were no "would have"s or "should have"s in martial arts. I looked at him as if seeing him for the first time. "Thank you," I said.

≈

Following the test, I was given a two-sword ceremony (and this time, my mother attended). Jack presented me with my certificate and belt, and the guys in the class shook my hand and bowed. I had learned from Sifu that bowing was important because it kept a person humble, but I had never understood, until now, why it was so important to remain humble.

I tried to imagine what Jack would have been like if he had not gotten so caught up in his own power. I had occasionally seen glimpses of the younger Jack who was no doubt humble and eager to learn, the more naive Jack, the more compassionate man I knew must have existed. When I saw this gentle side of him, the chasm between who he was and who he thought he was narrowed. As I gained his respect and as he, therefore, lowered himself down from his own pedestal, I saw the humanity in him, the person he could have been. A part of me loved that part of him—if only it had not been so hard to get to most of the time. Ultimately, however, being around Jack was not worth the danger. I had achieved my goal and was already on my way out.

In the months that followed my black-belt test, I frequented the dojo less often. I had begun teaching for Jack when I was a brown belt, and I kept a few students under my tutelage, visiting the dojo at least long enough to complete their classes.

But like most martial arts students, they quit a few months into the practice, and when I was left with no students to teach, my dojo visits trickled to nothing. I stopped by now and then to watch a class, to see Jack's new initiates, maybe to wish them well on the incredible journey I knew they would take with Jack. But it was like walking back into a dream of darkness after you've awakened. The intensity of the emotion is no longer there, but the substance of fear is always available. Fear does not leave.

Still, I did not regret having dreamed the dream; for what-

ever reason, it had been necessary for my particular psychological makeup. It had made it clear to me that I *could* do those
sorts of things, if necessary—if, for example, an all-out war
broke out in my backyard. Of course, I had no illusion that I
had actually been through anything as horrifying as war with
Jack. But I had the certainty that human wholeness is complex
and inextricable from humility. It is the light casting across
mountains on a fall day. The curtain of rain that darkens the
scene. The awareness of the curved beauty of the world that
relies on both shadows and light.

LEARNING FEAR

Friday night and the gals and I are driving around, doing nothing but being teenagers. Vicki and Laura are sitting in the front seat, smoking cigarettes, while I'm hanging my head out the back window because the ashy-sharp scent burns my nose. My eyes water as the cool, dry wind smacks my eyeballs. Laura is driving. She's sixteen, blond, Italian, pretty. Stevie Wonder's singing, "You are the sunshine of my life" on the radio, and Vicki, the oldest of us, already pregnant at seventeen, is drinking a Pepsi, flicking the ash off her Kool. We're laughing so loudly we can barely hear the music, and then we're suddenly quiet, so quiet there's time enough for me to notice that the layered silhouette of the mountains against the fading blue sky is beautiful, the tenacity of daylight holding on against the darkness that inevitably falls. Laura Deloria and I have known each other since first grade, and although my family has moved about while hers has remained here in Colorado, I have always considered her my best friend, even during the years when we never spoke. I have little in common with Laura now other than this, the distant love we share, a recognition of time passed. That's what I'm thinking when a truckload of guys pulls up next to us and Vicki, for no reason, rolls down the window, bats her eyes, and says sweetly to the football player closest to her, "Excuse me, sir. Do you suffer from impotence?"

Laura's eyes light like the flash of a camera—everything frozen for that second. The guys in the truck roar, words but none of them comprehensible, all of them obscene; then Laura peels out, tires screeching, back end fishtailing. She runs a red light and cuts off onto Lookout Mountain Road, a steep thing that coils skinny as a whip up the side of a mountain. She and Vicki are laughing, but it doesn't seem like laughter to me. They're clenching their teeth, lips pulled taut, eyelids propped open like puppets', and they're so giddy I can almost see the nerves underneath their skin, feel the electric current pumping through their bodies like hot sparks.

I'm sitting in the backseat, and when Vicki asks her question, I laugh a little bit, too. It's funny, the randomness of it all when you're sixteen and the world won't make sense no matter how you twist it; still, I know Vicki should not have done what she did. When I see headlights bouncing in our rearview mirror, swerving from one side of the narrow, sinuous road to the other, I *really* know she shouldn't have done it.

"Are they following us?" Laura says incredulously.

Vicki looks back, and their laughter recharges, like an engine downshifting to pick up speed. "Sheeee-it." Their words are mock fear, all in fun.

But that changes. We're nearing the top of the mountain and the 1967 Chevy Nova we're driving is too clunky, too fatigued to make this feel anything like the very cool high-speed chase Laura and Vicki are pretending. We're going thirty-five, fifteen on the horseshoes, and the truck is tailgating us, the guys in it quiet now, not leaning out the window, not playing any games, and Vicki and Laura are no longer laughing. They're worried.

Laura pulls out a cigarette, lights it with the red-hot coils of the car lighter, inhales. "Shit," she says, a whisper, no mockery this time. Her eyes cast upward to the rearview mirror.

"Are they still there?" Vicki says.

Laura nods, her eyes skittish, going from mirror to road to mirror.

We're coming to a scenic overlook with a small parking area. I say, "Stop the car."

"What?" Laura says.

"Pull over and stop the car."

Vicki turns all the way around in her seat to glare at me. "Fucking crazy." She looks back at Laura and rolls her eyes. "She thinks she can fucking beat them up."

"I didn't say that." I can feel the tension in my gut, the frustration.

Laura snorts, because this is what she and Vicki hate about me, that I do martial arts and don't smoke pot or cigarettes, and already I'm teaching a martial arts class at a private high school. They want nothing to do with my goody-goody, health-nut, oh-so-philosophical bullshit, and just as I'm thinking this, the truck goes from tailgating to bumping us. We feel the slight jolt, enough to steer us off course for a split second, which would be enough on this skinny road to send us flying over the edge of the mountain. I see the water welling in Laura's eyes, but no tears fall. "Fuck," she says, her voice suddenly dry. She pulls over, shifts into neutral, then turns around in her seat and looks at me, desperate, angry, pleading.

≈

Before we left tonight, I was hanging out with Laura at her place. She has a pool—unheard of in our little cracker-box suburb, where front yards consist of tufts of grass in dry dirt, the whole area cluttered with Big Wheels, car transmissions, and stacks of old tires. Any day of the week, you can see fathers sitting in lawn chairs under their carports, radios tuned to Bronco high-lights. They don't move, other than to sip their iced tea or beer. But Laura's parents are different. They're real partyers; they spend their money on fun rather than necessity, and as far as most high school kids are concerned, Laura's house is the place to be. Her parents are active in the community—PTA, church barbecues, Sunday afternoon softball, and because her mother is the Avon lady, people frequent their house, strangers who become friends because Laura's mother, a woman with dark auburn hair and a Lois Lane body, is sweet and gracious. "Thank you. Come again," she says.

"Thank you, Norma. Thanks for the iced tea, too."

Laura is allowed to smoke in the house. She is allowed to say "bullshit," and "fuck." She has cool parents.

As we were getting ready to leave that night, her father was hanging out by the pool, leaning on the cheap umbrella table, sipping a cocktail. It was not his first for the day. He wore a Hawaiian shirt and shorts in an effort to be suave, but with his bony legs and long face, he looked like Pinocchio on a tropical vacation. Laura and I were just getting out of the pool, and she stopped for a minute to talk to him. "Can I use the car tonight?" she said.

"Where you going?"

"Out."

The smart-aleck answer that every teenager gives bothered Laura's father—I could see it in his eyes—but he said nothing. He just turned and gazed at the pool, lazily, as if he were rich and had all the time in the world. Then slowly, smooth as a Vegas lounge singer, his arm reached out toward Laura. She was wearing her swimsuit, and her father tucked his first two fingers into the cup of her bra, feeling her breast.

"You need money?" he said.

Laura pulled back and pushed her father's hand away, using less force than she wanted to, I could tell by the weakness of her gesture, the strength of her anger. Her whole body was afraid, though she stiffened and looked tough. She said, "Dad."

Her father retreated like a shunned boyfriend who knew he would get what he wanted in private. He handed her a twenty and the keys. He laughed a little.

≋

The headlights flood the car like an interrogation, then go dark. It's pitch-black up here, the stars like holes torn in a blanket of night, the light of heaven shining through, if you believe in heaven. If you don't, it's just a black dome specked with light that is already history, the distance creating a chasm you could never cross. And it is silent.

The guys don't close the doors as they get out, and the beat-up, powder-blue Ford looks winged, too heavy to fly. There are four of them, and for a moment I wonder how all those guys were crammed into the cab of that truck. Then my mind clicks into its everyday mode; I size them up. One guy is skinny, probably not considered a good fighter, but his arms are as long as a monkey's. He's wiry, and I know he's probably more powerful than he thinks he is. Another guy, the obvious tough guy of the bunch, is huge, solid as a canned ham, and top-heavy. His legs are too skinny and he locks his knees with every step. He's an easy target, and I am not one to wait. If I hear a noise outside when I'm sleeping, I put on my shoes and go check it out. Once, when an obscene phone caller whispered into the receiver all that he wanted to do to me, I gave him my address—no threats, just my address. Then I went out and sat on my front lawn. He never showed. No unfamiliar cars drove by. My mom and dad were angry, told me I was crazy, but I liked to get things over with. The whispering voice never called again.

These guys, however, are not on the end of the phone line. They are laughing as they walk toward us. But their laughter surprises me. They don't beeline toward our car; they swagger, swig their beers, take their time. I draw a deep breath, and a certain sort of relief washes over me. They're not bent on hurting us, not really. They feel obligated because their pride's been hurt—and they half-believe Vicki's provocative question was a come-on by a bad girl who really wanted them to follow her. They might be half right, but when you're seventeen and pregnant, you don't always know what you want. All these thoughts run through my head in a few seconds, because they are not really thoughts but, rather, the way my body responds to danger without thinking. It has become involuntary, this sizing up, the assessment of the risk and the quickest way to skirt it. And this time, I realize, we *can* skirt it. I look at Laura and say, "Floor it!"

She stutters to say something, but I interrupt.

"Pull a U-ey, then floor it!"

Laura wastes no time. In a minute we're flying down the

road we had crawled up seconds earlier. The guys from the truck scatter like pool balls to get out of our way, and Laura and Vicki find this hilarious. They're laughing again, hooting louder than ever now.

I'm sitting with my head propped on the backseat between them, peering out the windshield. There's a turnout behind some bushes, and I tell Laura to pull off and cut the lights.

"What the fuck?" Vicki says.

Laura does what I say.

"What the fuck? Fucking stupid. No, Laura, keep going."

When the truckload of guys passes us, Laura laughs, a real laugh this time. Her brown eyes catch mine in the rearview mirror, a kind of thanks that doesn't need words. Vicki turns quiet. We pull out and follow the distant taillights of the Ford down Lookout Mountain, James Taylor singing that sweet lullaby to himself, and no way for any of us to turn around on this tight mountain road.

≈

At school Laura and I have become estranged. I carry a book in my back pocket and read whenever possible—lunch, study hall, mandatory assemblies—and Vicki and Laura make fun of me whenever possible. When they retell the story of what happened Friday night, it goes like this:

Laura picks me up before school, and Vicki and her friend

Cindy are already smoking a joint. Cindy hands the stogie to me, obligatorily, and as usual I decline.

"She's too good for us," Vicki says. She glares at me. "'Bout got us killed the other night."

"What?" Cindy says.

"Thought she was all hot shit with her karate crap. Got us to the top of Lookout Mountain, four guys after us, and she tells Laura to pull over, like she's going to take them on."

Cindy's eyes go wide. "Did you?"

I shake my head no.

"No fuckin way. She couldn't. Chickened out, so we had to speed down the mountain at the last minute."

"What about the guys?"

"They passed us, went on their way."

I haven't known Cindy all my life. She's Vicki's best friend in the way I am Laura's, since first grade. Still, Cindy seems disappointed in me, and it's hard not to let this get under my skin. I want to say, "That wasn't karate, but it *was* martial arts. The whole thing is about staying cool enough to *not* fight, Vicki." I want to say it with a sneer, but I know it would just set me up for more of Vicki's anger, which is unending and has nothing to do with me. I keep my mouth shut. Cindy shrugs, closes her eyes, and rests her head on the open window. The wind tangles her long, dark hair.

When we get to school, Laura, Vicki, and Cindy run ahead of me because Adam Dupree, recently voted "Best Hair" (better than being a star quarterback in the early seventies) is standing at the school entrance, waving to them. I watch my friends run ahead of me. At noon, I will be able to leave school in order to teach my class at the private high school. Already, I'm looking forward to the lunch bell ringing.

≈

I have a picture of Laura and me that was taken in first grade: we are beaming at the camera, and our blond hair falls in curls around our shoulders in a manner I have seen only on dolls. It is out of place, our hair, because it is perfectly well behaved, and we are anything but. Our eyes squint at the camera, not with fear or to hide from the bright flash but because our smiles are so broad we cannot help but squint. We are holding hands and kneeling in front of three other kids, whose gazes meander to the borders of the photo. Our free hands make fists, not for fighting but as if we have joined in an effort to rein in the excitement that is pulling us gently but firmly through this remarkable life. We look like we should be in a pop-up book, instead of flat on the page. We're holding back that much energy.

The photo is a still shot that embodies, for me, my entire childhood friendship with Laura. From first to third grade, we shared the same classes at school. We did well in our studies, but we talked too much—mostly to each other. During recess, we usually stayed inside, writing, "I will not talk. I will not talk."

We shared secrets, made pacts, swore we would remain forever friends.

When we did make it to recess, we played four-square, a game at which Laura excelled. She was a good athlete, a competitive kid who, one day, used her hard-earned winnings in four-square to declare that, for a week, Wilfred Yost would be the leader of all games. Wilfred was the school's whipping post. His clothes were always torn, and he picked his nose with less abashedness than most of us. But for a week, he was king of the court, by Laura's command, and everyone obeyed. She was well liked, smart as a whip, fast on her feet, determined.

When I returned to Colorado in high school, I anticipated my first meeting with Laura. We would go into her bedroom and talk for hours; I'd hear about her boyfriends and tell her about mine, and I'd tell her about my experiences with Sifu, how important that relationship—and martial arts—had become to me.

The meeting went nothing like I had anticipated.

We did scream and hug and do all the things good girlfriends do when they haven't seen each other for a long time, and we did sit in Laura's bedroom, catching up on old times. But ten minutes into our conversation, her eyes drooped, then wandered, lighting on nothing, no interest, no passion. We were sitting on the floor and, lethargically, she twisted around and opened the drawer of her nightstand. She pulled out a compact mirror, lines of coke sparkling like the tail of a shooting star.

Her eyes lit up. She looked at me impishly, the kid I knew in first grade. "You want some?"

I shook my head.

She pulled a rolled-up dollar bill from the same drawer, snorted two lines, cleaned the mirror with her finger, and rubbed the dregs along her gums. She shook her head like a woman getting out of a swimming pool, refreshed, revived. "They have good shit in L.A.?" she said. "I heard they have good shit out there."

It wasn't that I had never tried drugs. I had lived in L.A. in the late sixties, early seventies, when a single concert at the Forum could get you high—no chance of claiming you didn't inhale there. But everything I'd ever tried made me feel sick, or lethargic, or just plain stupid. I didn't get the draw, and when I told Laura that, she lost interest again. She looked around the room as I spoke. She fidgeted.

Oddly, as if our childhood pact had been chiseled on stone tablets, we kept seeing each other daily. Though we learned right away that time had erased any interests we might have once shared, we continued to share our secrets.

A month or so into our awkward, struggling friendship, Laura told me her biggest secret. We were in her room again, and she was smoking a Kool. We had plans to go out that night, but she was dragging her feet. I said, "We don't have to go if you don't want to."

"I want to." She sat in one place.

"We could stay here, hang out by the pool."

"It's my father. He doesn't really want me to go."

"I thought he said it was okay."

"It is okay. He said it was okay. It's just, he makes me sleep with him."

"What?"

"He makes me have sex with him if I want to go out. If I want to drive the car, anything." She was speaking in the same tone of voice my other friends used when they said things like "My dad won't let me go to all-night parties," "My mom won't let me drive," "My parents want me to get all A's." "My father makes me have sex with him"—as if whatever takes place within your own family is the benchmark for what is normal, acceptable, unescapable.

I don't remember how I responded. My memory fades to black when I recall the moment. I remember Laura telling me that Mitsy, her older sister, had gone through the same thing— her father raped her when she asked for permission to do anything; it was the family rule. I learned that Vicki's father sexually abused her, too, and to a certain extent, that's why Laura and Vicki had become such good friends.

Laura and I didn't go out that night. Instead, I spent the night at Laura's house. I didn't want to leave her alone. We talked until way past midnight, then she took four or five Valium and went to sleep. I lay there awake, angry, frustrated, wondering how I could be her friend now. I wasn't considering breaking our childhood pact; I was trying to figure out how to be a real friend, someone who could get her out of this situation, how to stop her pain. When I came up with nothing, no solution, I tried to forget about it. But it was like a splinter of glass underneath my skin. I forgot it was there until I moved a certain way; then the thing dug in deeper.

After Laura told me, I began to see it happening. (Was it there before and I did not see it, or had her father grown lazy about hiding it?) Mr. Deloria was shockingly indiscreet, as if he had a right or, sometimes, as if he was making an example of Laura, and daring me to object. He knew I had studied martial arts, and he made it clear that he found the notion of a woman being able to defend herself against a man silly and inane. "I've got a black belt, too," he'd say. "And I'm not afraid to use it when I have to." He eyed Laura. I had grown to hate the sight of him, which put an extra strain on my friendship with Laura.

≈

Things fell apart in the most fascinating ways back then. The day yearbook photos were being taken, Adam Dupree, "Best Hair," arrived on campus with a completely bald head, shiny as a cue ball. Then, after school, he asked me to a party at Laura's house. It was an unprecedented act: I was an unknown, the martial arts geek; he was a star.

Adam and I arrived at Laura's place stylishly late. Her father greeted us at the door and handed us both a beer. Mr. Deloria was popular with the kids, a good all-around guy, a father who would dance with us and not tell us to turn down the volume when Robert Plant sounded like he was spitting pieces of his lungs into the speakers.

To this day, I sometimes wish I had been raised Catholic. I would then have understood the significance of the Saint Christopher medals my friends exchanged with one another back then; and I might have understood the famous quote that asks God to grant us the serenity to accept the things we can not change, the courage to change the things we can, and the wisdom to know the difference. It was a serenity I did not possess when I was sixteen.

The party was a big hit. Mr. Deloria had rented a mirrored disco ball and hung it on a cable above the pool. The red, yellow, and green floodlights that normally lit the area like a cheap Hawaiian luau refracted off the ball—very cool and psychedelic. On the concrete patio, kids danced in front of a strobe light, their silhouettes flickering like disjointed still frames of a black-and-white movie. Kids smoked pot, French-kissed each other at random, no parents to stop them. We drank beer. We cursed like adults. It was fun.

Adam Dupree was the social magnet, as usual, this time not because of his hair but because of his lack of it. People surrounded him and asked him if they could touch his head. They took bets on whether or not it was a joke—maybe Adam had donned a skullcap for the day of pictures and the whole thing was a fake. As caring as Adam tried to be toward me, I ended up taking a backseat to his popularity, and eventually I slipped inside the house, hoping maybe I could help Mrs. Deloria bring out more pretzels or pizza.

The Deloria house always smelled a little foul to me, a combination of stale cigarette smoke, booze, and a bevy of toy dachshunds that Mrs. Deloria raised and sold. Save for the dachshunds, asleep in their crates, the place was empty. A dim, sallow light, like pus, lit the kitchen. On the linoleum table sat several bowls of Fritos, Bugles, sour-cream dip, and a pink-and-white sheet cake. I sat down, away from the crowd, rejuvenating my slender extroverted tendencies before I went back out to the party. I was having a good time, but I just needed some quiet before I had more of a good time.

I leaned back in my chair, sighed, and closed my eyes. That's when I heard a slight whimper, coming from the darkened living room. I tried to tell myself it was one of the dogs, but I knew before I opened my eyes what was happening. I knew Mr. Deloria had not seen me sitting there in the darkness; I knew the sound was Laura's voice.

I stood up and walked toward the living room. There, I saw the silhouette of Mr. Deloria's face lit eerily by the moon. Laura's back was to me, and he was looking over her shoulder, his body pressed too close to hers. I couldn't see exactly what was happening, nor did I try. I did not want to know the specifics.

I was frozen. I didn't know whether to leave or to confront him. I couldn't figure out which would be best for Laura. Before I made my decision, Mr. Deloria walked toward me, guilt-less, charming, as if nothing had happened. "You having a good time?" He smiled.

I tried to answer. I couldn't.

"Everybody else is out having a good time. What are you, the wallflower of the bunch? Poor thing. Can't get a guy to give you what you need?"

"Dad, come on," Laura said.

He chuckled and headed for the patio, and I thought it would be over. But before he got to the door, he stopped. He looked at me. "You need a little—" He grabbed Laura between the legs and held on for a minute. "Doesn't she, Laura?" He let go of her crotch. He laughed again. Not meanly, but as if he really was joking around, as if he believed Laura was in on the joke with him and I was the odd person out, the loser goody-goody who did not see the fun.

I said, "You're a fucking sick fuck."

He cocked his head and smiled, surprised.

Laura looked at me. "It's okay," she said, first to me, then to her dad. "It's okay."

"It is not okay." I looked at her dad. "You sick, sick fuck. You keep your fucking hands off her."

He laughed again. Then he approached me and started to grab my crotch, just as he had done to Laura.

I didn't think; it was reflex. With one hand, I twisted his wrist and sent him to his knees. It happened in seconds. And then Laura came at me.

"Stop it," she said, protecting him, pushing me back, hard.

I looked at Mr. Deloria, confusion whirring through my body. I imagined myself going back at him, applying the wrist hold harder, a smidge short of the point at which I knew his wrist would snap and his ligaments would tear. It's what I wanted to do. Just then, he looked as if he would come at me again, and I stood there, wishing he would. I glanced at Laura. She held her arms out to both sides, keeping me from her dad. He did not come at me again.

Laura started screaming. "Get out of the house, get out now, you fucking bitch, leave now!" Kids started coming in from the patio to see what the noise was all about. Mr. Deloria was up from the floor now. He was trying to swagger again, mingling among the teenagers, joking, telling them nothing was wrong, I'd lost it—and wasn't I a little bit off to begin with, the weird girl they didn't need at their party anyway.

I kept looking at Laura for any sign that would let me know she had been faking it, she was not really mad at me, she was mad at her dad. Nothing. Her anger was impenetrable. It was all directed at me.

I left the party, left Adam without a date, and I walked home. I walked across the field where Laura and I had once played, the place where we had built a secret fort, our refuge every summer until we were eight. In that fort, we had pricked our fingers with needles, pressed our hands together, and swore blood sisters forever. I missed her, the girl I knew then, the friend I'd come back for.

≈

The walls of any high school ooze. When you're a kid that age, there's no getting around it. The minute you walk through those double doors, all life changes. It could be that you like the person you become inside the high school walls better than the person "on the outside." Perhaps you're a star jock, or the prom queen. More likely, however, the walls scream your weaknesses, the ways in which *you* are *different.*

Monday morning, I walked to school (Laura didn't call to confirm that she'd pick me up as usual), and when I entered, the walls were oozing my name. Within seconds I learned that Adam Dupree had tried to kiss me at Laura's party, and that I had responded by grabbing his balls—not in an amorous manner. After assaulting Adam, I had left the party.

As I walked from one class to the other, it was like the parting of the Red Sea. My peers split off into groups, everyone keeping a good distance from me. When I saw Adam across the hallway, he glared at me, as if it had really happened, as if he had really tried to kiss me and I had fought him off. I didn't know if he was going along with the story to protect Laura, or if he was angry at me for leaving without him and had to make up a reason. Or maybe he thought *I* had made up the story. The power of mass media pales in comparison to the power of high school gossip.

≈

When I look back on the incident, I am sometimes overwhelmed with remorse. When I reacted to Mr. Deloria's aggression, I did not take into consideration that Laura would have to remain there, at the party. She would have to give her guests an explanation of why she had become so angry at me. When the party was over, she would have to go to sleep in her bedroom, footsteps away from her father's bedroom. Incest was not a household word then, as it is today. No one would have believed Laura's story.

Other times, when I look back, I am overwhelmed with satisfaction. To ignore his savage act would have meant denying my sense of self, submitting to the hollowness of his assumed power. I had stood up for myself, and I had shown that Mr. Deloria could not get away with his behavior forever. Laura, like me, had the strength to fight off his attacks. Perhaps it was selfish, but I wanted her to know that.

I did not realize at the time that my act had been so utterly revolutionary that it would cause a permanent dent in how my high school peers perceived me. Somehow, the story had been twisted so far from the truth, and somehow, Adam Dupree was not made fun of for having his balls grabbed by a girl. As the story went, I put him to his knees, not because he was weak but because I was a freak. I was stronger than I was supposed to be. Adam had to submit because I was a girl who was not really a girl—and I had certainly not been elevated to the power of a guy—so I was somewhere in between. A genderless monster. It was not just the case of Laura's father that had created this image of me. It was the fact that I sometimes walked down streets alone at night, or went to a movie alone, or stopped and helped a *guy* who was stuck by the side of the road—as if I had the right. It was the fact that I was the same as I had been when we were all boys and girls playing four-square on the playground; I had not grown up. I had not learned how to be constantly—subconsciously—submissive and afraid. I was not a woman.

I once heard the stand-up comic Elayne Boosler put it in a nutshell. In her bit, she says, "My boyfriend asked me to meet him down by the pier after the show tonight." As she delivers this line, her jaw drops with utter incredulity. She continues. "I said, 'Down by the pier'? 'Down by the pier'?! I can't meet you down by the pier! It's dark. I have a dress on. I have my vagina with me." The audience roars with laughter. "Tell you what, I'll leave my vagina at home, or in my other purse. *Then* I'll meet you down by the pier."

It is the perfect comedy—an observation of daily life that, when exposed, makes us all a little nervous. So we laugh. After all, it is absurd. A part of a person's body truly should not be a liability.

But this is what young women learn. The transition from girlhood to womanhood includes the lingering awareness that you can be raped. True, a boy or girl of any age can be raped. But the chances increase exponentially for women, and it's not just the *chances* that increase, it's the constant awareness of fear.

As a young woman, you learn that you cannot, ever again, walk down to the pier, carefree as a child. You cannot leave your vagina in your other purse.

But there is a different way to see it. A woman, like a female (or male) of any species, has within her the proclivity for fierceness and a heightened sense of self-preservation. In nature, no matter how violent the mating process becomes, the purpose remains to bear offspring. Rape does not hold this purpose; rape is about power. Hatred of females is something that is learned by the only animal who, according to scientists, has a mind. And so it can be unlearned. So can the fear.

≈

At the end of that first week after the incident, when school ended, I felt somehow relieved. I had made it through all the harassment and ostracism. I knew the gossip would continue, but I knew I could withstand it. As I walked up to my front door, my mother greeted me. "You haven't been riding with Laura recently," she observed.

"Nah. I like the walk."

My mother probably saw through my nonchalance, but she asked no questions, just went about our regular routine. Religiously, when I returned home from school, she would read off the names of self-defense techniques or forms I was learning, and I would perform the corresponding moves.

When we were done, I would take a nap, wake up, have a

piece of ginseng, a tablespoon of peanut butter, and a table-spoon of honey for dinner, and then take off for my martial arts class. My mother did not like that I ate peanut butter and ginseng for dinner. She did not like that I often came home bruised and injured from sparring. She did not like that I was out every night at the dojo until well past bedtime. However, she saw that the study of martial arts was making me a strong woman, a confident person. Nightly, and every weekend morning, she handed me the car keys and said, "Have a good class." It was one of the best gifts she could have given me.

≈

I did not talk to Laura again until the last month of our senior year. I was walking across "our field," and between then and now, it had become a baseball diamond, bright green grass crisscrossed with lawn mower marks, the chain-link fence of the backstop cast in a pinkish hue reflecting off twilight clouds. The whole place was conspicuous in its absence of noise—no crowd cheering, no crack of a bat, no smell of hot dogs and taffy. I was looking at the sunset the way you look when you know you'll be leaving. I would graduate soon. I planned to return to Los Angeles—hopefully to see Sifu again—and the prospect made the jagged mountains seem a little softer, more forgiving. After a while, I heard voices behind me, the sound suspended in the hollow air above open land. The people were laughing—no harm, no reason to turn around.

A few minutes later though, I heard footsteps walking too close behind me. I turned. It was Laura. She had split off from the crowd. She said, "Hi."

I felt like I was planning a dissertation in my head—that's how long it took me to say, "Hi." I wished in that moment that she were walking up to me to say, "Thanks, things are better now"—as if her situation could just miraculously get better. I wished we were both what we had been in that photo of us in first grade, two kids not easily contained, every choice in the world in front of us, nothing we could not choose, and so much energy.

"You walking?" she said.

I laughed a little, looked down at my feet. "Yeah, I'm walking."

"Where you going?"

I shrugged. "Home."

Her face was red. She would not look back at the people behind us, their voices still hanging in the hollow air. I sensed a longingness, a part of her that, like me, would not easily let go of that pact we had made as children. "You want to walk home with me?" she said.

I didn't need any words. I just stopped, turned around, and started walking toward her place.

Whatever we said to each other in the fifteen minutes or so it took us to get to her house was inconsequential. An occasional "How you been?" A nod. Some laughter that was anything but.

A few doors from her home, she stopped. She said, "You staying here after you graduate?"

I shrugged. "Don't know yet. You?"

"Got a job." She smiled. "Hundred bucks a week. Got an apartment. I'm moving out."

I wanted to hug her. I said, "Good. That's really good."

Then, for no reason, she reached out and touched my shoulder. It was an awkward gesture that held within it all our attempts to hold on to the way we believed things should be, the affection we once shared and wanted to continue to share, the expectations we had held for each other when we were kids, our fond anticipation of growing up, and the actual horrors (and satisfactions) that growing up had brought to us. She said, "Take care, will you?"

I nodded. "You do the same."

She turned away before I did. I watched her walk down the street and turn the corner toward her house.

≈

I don't know for sure what was going on that day in the field. I heard stories about it—that Laura (who had gotten a reputation for sleeping around) had slapped a boy in the face when he got fresh with her.

"What did she expect?" people said. "She asked for it, she got it." The usual insightful teenage bullshit.

When they asked me about it, I stumbled. When the twelfth person of the day began grilling me with questions, I said, out of nowhere, "You know, Laura Deloria could kick your ass in four-square."

The guy looked at me as if I was crazy, because I was. I would not succumb, and in the end, I knew Laura would not succumb. I had seen it in her when she was a child. Whatever had happened that day in the field, it seemed clear that she had stood up for herself when others had expected her to give in. She was crazy. And good for her.

"I got a job. I got an apartment," she said. Because he did not win. Her life up till then should have been different. It wasn't. But it would be.

"She could kick your ass in four-square." I was downright, happily, self-confidently crazy. I was a girl in high school, and although I did not assume I would always win, I knew I always had a fighting chance.

THE THRUM OF THE WORLD:
A MEDITATION ON MEDITATION

Some things happen for reasons, others do not. There is a beauty in chaos, an asymmetry that denies logic. I do not wish to live in a world that has been fully explained. I enjoy the thrum of the world.

One day, when I was in my early thirties and living on my own in California, my house fell down in an earthquake. I had many things in the house—clothes, a computer, books, papers, family photographs—but the earth shook, and the house and everything in it fell into the ravine that existed before the house was built on the ravine. So there was one beginning.

I moved from that house (now a ravine) into a series of temporary homes until, three months later, when the earthquake aftershocks had quit rumbling in me and around me, I found a pink-and-white home on East Cliff Avenue in Santa Cruz, California. A friend of a friend of a friend had said to me, "Go see the Zen priest who lives in the yellow-and-white house on West Cliff Avenue." And when I went to see the Zen priest, we liked each other, and she said, "The house next door is for rent. Why don't you take it?"

It was a beautiful place, more beautiful because of the ocean nearby and the uncertainty of the home's stability. (It could fall into that great sea at any time. What remains after an earthquake is what was there to begin with.) And so, since the pink-and-white house was filled with light, another uncertainty, the way it comes and goes, and yet scientists say it is eternal, I said to the Zen priest, "Yes, I want to live in this house. I will take it."

After I moved in, I heard sirens one night. They rode the waves of the sea, drilling into my ears, as sirens will do sometimes when you live by the sea and are used to hearing only that hush. The house was small, my bedroom too small for a bed *and* a lamp, and so I went without the lamp. That darkness made the red and blue police lights all the more like a bruise replacing the night sky that usually hung so pretty on the other side of my window. I looked out. Police officers were walking to Natasha's house in that bruise of light. Natasha was the Zen priest, and she and I had shared wine, had dined together, become good friends. The police did not come out of Natasha's house for some time. No ambulance came. Later, the red and blue lights turned off, and the police officers drove away. They had some paperwork to do. Someone had broken into Natasha's house. It was a man. He had found Natasha sleeping in her bed and put his hand over her mouth. He had said, "I am going to rape you."

Natasha was a sixty-five-year-old survivor of breast cancer. She had not had reconstructive surgery. I wonder what the man would have thought if he'd seen her chest, a map of scars that marked her strength, her will to live.

He did not see her chest.

Weeks later, I was at Natasha's house having dinner. We were talking, and she explained to me that the young man who had broken in was someone she had known and trusted, someone she had hired to help her with her yard chores—the lawn, the garden. He had been unemployed, and she had been compassionate. She had hired him and paid him weekly. She had gotten to know him. When she woke from sleep that night, he was already there, on top of her.

She called it *presence of mind*. She said, "I had been meditating for so many years. I was not about to lose myself to this." Waking from sleep, pinned, she was able to fight him off.

She had no martial arts training. None. I don't know the specifics—only that Natasha had remained unharmed.

Meditation.

≋

Some schools of martial arts teach physical self-defense. Perhaps there is a triangle on the wall. Perhaps the triangle says

Perhaps the teacher is a "grandmaster" (which means, simply, a teacher who has taught other teachers). In a ninety-minute class, ten minutes will be devoted to meditation. People have to get their money's worth. How can you demonstrate your powerful and impressive skills of meditation to your friends? How can you test for the next level of consciousness? How do you even know there are levels of consciousness? Perhaps there's just one, and it never goes away. But you go away from it.

Spar.

Kata / form.

Drills.

Spar.

Kata / form.

Drills.

If you have a creative teacher, there are other innovations in between. But this is the usual regime.

Perhaps it is easier for men to learn to fight without presence of mind. Though it's doubtful to me that *all* men are better fighters than *all* women (or vice versa), I do believe the fight comes from a different place inside the two genders.

Most martial arts schools are run by men. And so.

≈

I have rarely met a girl or a woman who seeks to learn martial arts in order to impress people, to get a better physique, to learn to fight better on the playground, or to get a boyfriend. Women learn martial arts with the goal of *not* fighting. There's something pure about this; it is not a Zen koan or a Daoist paradox. In order to feel safe, a woman must learn to fight. And in so doing, she becomes aware of what is natural to her before culture imposes timidity and submissiveness upon her. It's about self-preservation. It's about self-esteem.

Physical training, self-discipline, a certain amount of gymnastic skill, and inner and outer strength—these are the basic requirements of martial arts. However, if you rely solely on these things you will be only equal to your prowess at these things. So will your opponent. Presence of mind is key.

≈

While I was in high school, I taught martial arts at an all-girls Catholic school. As usual, there was one student who took to what I was teaching more profoundly than the others. On a few occasions, she visited the private dojo where I taught. She considered becoming a student, but she was a devout Catholic and could not understand why meditation was a part of martial arts.

"You concentrate on emptying your mind, and idleness is the devil's workshop," she said.

I said, "Why don't you try it once, see what you think? Saint Francis of Assisi was big on meditation."

She would not try. She would not allow herself to turn off the chatter in her mind. She was a good person, a smart person. But she could not meditate, and it ended her pursuit of martial arts training, an activity she loved.

I wondered why it was taboo to her. Was the source of her daily, un-idle mind chatter divine? Or are we afraid of the power that comes from stillness? My mind chatter is a TV commercial. Slogans I don't care about appear in the vapors of my brain: "Dodge trucks are ram tough." Songs I have never listened to in my life show up in my head. Somehow I know that you should call Janet Jackson Miss Jackson, if you're nasty. My mind is like a lint trap. When not meditating, my mind is a workshop for the most vacuous and idle aspects of my culture.

In silence, I hear my own thoughts. And eventually, I hear nothing. "The Dao that can be spoken of is not the eternal Dao." The Jewish name for God, which cannot be said aloud, YHWH.

≈

I lived in New York City for a brief period of my life, so brief I never got used to it. I always felt as if the jaws of the city were closing down on me, as if I were riding a bicycle, fast, my head turned over my shoulder, staring at the saliva-drenched uvula of some grand reptile, its teeth, the buildings surrounding me, its tongue, the road beneath my tires. I didn't stand a chance.

I had been hired to assist a famous chef because of my martial arts skills, so I had a decent job. I did not understand the connection the chef saw between cooking and martial arts, but he asked me to wear my gi to my interview. Quirky. New York. So I wore my gi and he hired me on the spot. I started work that afternoon, wage, ten bucks an hour. I thought it was good.

Daily I rode the subway from the East Side to the West Side, sometimes at two A.M. Often, I would walk down Forty-second Street at that late hour. On these nights, I was followed more than once. I don't know if the men or women following me wanted to sell me drugs, rob me, or ask me for some lewd sexual favor. And I use the word "ask" loosely.

But one day I left work early, around noon, and I decided to stroll around the city. As I walked, I felt accosted, as I almost always felt in New York. There were things I loved about the city, but I never truly got used to it. I needed a frequent reprieve. As I rounded a corner, I found myself in smaller jaws, jaws inside the city's huge jaws, a great steel awning meant to protect me from the building construction taking place. So now, on top of the sirens, the taxis honking their horns incessantly, the people yelling at broken pay phones, and other people yelling at buses too full to carry them—on top of all that—there were hammers pounding, drills whining, some kind of high-pitched, chain-saw buzz.

I have a problem with sensory overload. I'm not good at taking in a million things at once. So when I looked up and saw the sign that said ZEN CENTER, I felt the city's magic—and the city does have a certain magic. The Zen Center appeared. Incense wafted into the street. Jasmine mixed with the city smells: gasoline, urine, and soot. Ahhhh. Like a piece of dust to a vacuum, I was sucked inside.

Refuge.

People were meditating already. They sat in rows, very organized. It seemed to be open meditation, because some people did not move for a long time, while others stood and left the building quietly, at random. There were small podiums in front of each meditation spot, and each held a book, its leaves spread open, kanji on the pages.

I wanted to sit right down, to start meditating immediately. But I was self-conscious; I did not know the appropriate procedure. At the front of the room sat a Japanese man with a shaved head; he was wearing an orange robe. I walked up to the orange-robed man. I said, "Is it okay if I meditate here?"

His eyes almost disappeared behind the pinched cheeks of his huge smile. He began laughing.

I became even more self-conscious. I said, "Is this a special group? Do I have to sign up or something?"

This one made the orange-robed man bust a gut.

I fidgeted. I turned around to see if I (or he) had disturbed the people who were meditating. They sat still as before, laughter falling around their ears.

I stood there awhile longer, looking for the right question. Then it dawned on me. He wanted a donation before I sat down. I reached into my pocket, pulled out a five-dollar bill, and pushed it his direction.

It did nothing to sober his mood. He had tears in the corners of his eyes by now. He was slapping his thighs.

I was growing frustrated and a little angry at his rudeness. They were legitimate questions. I was being polite. I thought to myself, *Well, screw this.* I shoved the five dollars back into my pocket, gave the guy an exasperated look, and took a place among the others. I began meditating—horns honking, chain saws buzzing, electric hammers exploding, sirens.

It was dusk by the time I left the building. I don't know what happened in there, but when I came out, the jaws of New York seemed a little softer, and I felt a little less like Dorothy chanting, "There's no place like home," the wee voice in the big city. New York was still there, but the beauty of the place shone through. The architecture. The bustle of people on the street. The sense of having somewhere to go. The magnificent history present on the surface of every building. The art on the streets—sculptures, glorious graffiti. The voices around me, the accents and dialects. A celebration. It felt good to me, like rain, because rain can either make you stir-crazy or crazy-happy. New York City: rain.

For the next month or so, until I left New York for good, I went back to that place every day. I never told anyone about it. I never talked to the orange-robed monk again, though, after a few visits, he began to acknowledge my presence when I entered.

Now, when I think of the ideal place to meditate, I think of New York City. As I meditated longer and longer at that mysterious little place barraged with sirens and construction and the general noise of people on the go, it no longer made much sense to me to go on a meditation retreat to some mountain getaway three hundred miles from the nearest town, a pastoral place full of peace, devoid of conflict. Because the point is to find meditation in the midst of *this,* the stress of how we have come to live today. The stillness in the constant stimulation. The silence. The attention. The calm at the eye of the storm.

I was reading an American short story recently, something from a literary journal. In it, one character says to the other, "You have to practice judo and karate several hours a day to be good at them. Who has the time? Buy a gun." It is a sentiment I've heard often about martial arts, and it strikes me as both arrogant and ignorant. Martial arts are not only about learning to defend yourself; they are about learning to respect yourself, deeply. In the process of learning to respect yourself, you learn to humble yourself before the vast expanse of time and history that has come before you, to value posterity, to be constantly aware of the ways in which you are connected to nature, *and* to value and effect self-preservation—but never at the expense of losing your self-respect or your respect for other humans and living things.

When I meditate, the thrum of the world rolls like a flock of drums through my bones. It's about presence of mind. It's about compassion. It is not about being holy. It is about being whole.

THE EVERYDAY HOUSEWIFE
AND HER MANY WEAPONS

My friends had warned me. My mother, fretting for my safety, had warned me. "I just don't think you should teach in Five Points, honey. It's too dangerous." When she found out I was teaching from seven to nine-thirty P.M., I think she quit sleeping altogether. "It's at night? Can't they run a class during the day?"

I was twenty years old, living in an apartment five miles away, but even over the phone wire, I could see my mother's face, creased with worry.

"Mom, if Five Points is dangerous, then the women there need self-defense. That's why I'm going."

Eventually, she gave in. "Well, I suppose it's okay. But be careful."

As I took the turn off the highway into downtown, I wasn't scared so much as curious. Five Points had taken on mythic proportions to me. Twenty years ago, it was the pocket of Denver to be avoided at all costs. If my friends were driving and they mistakenly took a turn in that direction, they'd frantically look for the nearest entrance ramp to put them back on the freeway, heading toward their safe, suburban homes. I halfway imagined the houses in Five Points would be like mud huts packed side by side, with scraps of aluminum pitched over their walls as a roof. I expected gunshots, grandmothers with fear in their eyes peering from windows, kids standing on street corners in gangs or running down the sidewalks screaming bloody murder.

When I arrived, I found the neighborhood was much like mine. The houses were about the same size but older, and each one was different, unlike the houses on my block, which were identical except for a few variations in color. Chain-link fences encircled the yards, and kids' toys lay scattered like constellations in the dirt. The streets were quiet, lined with trees that arched over the narrow blacktop like a nave.

I grabbed my gi from the backseat and walked to the large brick building on the corner, the church that the YWCA had rented for the eight-week class they'd hired me to teach.

Shortly after the women arrived and settled into the place, I began teaching. "Okay, let's start by seeing what sorts of things you carry with you in your purses that could be used as weapons," I said. In the women's self-defense classes I had taught in the suburbs, I'd found the students liked to forage through one another's purses, check out who had the best coupons and who used the most expensive perfume. It was always a good icebreaker.

The women stared at me blankly for a little bit, then slowly started rummaging through their purses, mumbling among themselves. It was a response I'd never seen before.

Finally, Mickey, a heavyset woman with a blond crew cut, looked up at me. "You know, we don't have to figure out how to use what we carry in our purses as weapons. We—well, most of us anyway—we carry weapons," she said. One by one, the women pulled out knives—some switchblades, some Buck knives—until a half dozen or so shiny blades were pointing toward me.

I said, "Well, yeah, those will work. Those will definitely work as weapons."

An Asian woman who did not carry a knife was so shy she could barely look up when she spoke. She had a scar running from the middle of one eyebrow through one eyelid and down to the bottom of her jaw. She said, "But I want, I want to be able, I *want to learn to*—" And she stopped. She pushed her palm toward the group and recoiled into herself, on the verge of tears.

The few women who did not carry weapons started explaining themselves like kids who had not done their home work. Charlene picked up her Afro comb and held the five metal prongs out like a knife. "I have used this before," she said.

"Oh, yes, that's a good one," I said quickly. "You see, Charlene has a comb and she could use it in a self-defense situation."

Charlene held her comb high. I felt as if I were swimming, taking breaths in between strokes. In my head, I started planning the accelerated self-defense course I would clearly have to begin teaching next week. For that evening, though, I stayed right on track. I taught the vulnerable areas of the body, some basic ways to apply that knowledge.

As I left the room at the end of the class, I heard my students chatting and laughing. "Hey, Sensei," one of them called. I turned around, assuming the woman was talking to me, though I had never asked anyone to call me Sensei. Mickey stood there smiling. "We're going out for a drink. Want to come?"

I forced a smile and shook my head. "Maybe next time," I said.

I left the place feeling perplexed. The whole of Five Points looked different to me now. I noticed the industrial silos I had not seen on the way in, the numerous train tracks I had to cross, the viaducts I had to pass under. As train whistles faded, I felt the street rumbling beneath my tires, a low vibration that sank into my gut. While my neighborhood had streetlamps glowing amber on every corner, this neighborhood had neon signs buzzing, flicking on and off—COORS, BUD—but no street-lamps anywhere. Coming into the place, I had prided myself on my open mind, but now I realized my "open mind" was just an expectation that all lives mirrored mine. On my way into Five Points, I wanted desperately to believe it would be just like my neighborhood, only in the city. While it wasn't the way my friends and mother had warned me it would be, it also was not "just like my neighborhood." I could have been Mister Rogers up there, putting on my sweater and telling my students it was a nice day. *Charlene has a comb, and she could use it in a self-defense situation.*

Throughout the next few weeks, I taught Mickey, Charlene, and the rest of the class the basic punches and kicks, the theories and applications of self-defense techniques, and the meditation necessary for presence of mind.

About four weeks into class, however, Mickey quit coming. I asked the other women about her, but they knew nothing, and the other students were a little less engaged without Mickey there. She had been our source of comic relief. The night I'd brought in a group of male volunteers to act as model muggers, for instance, Mickey had brought a rubber face mask of President Nixon. When a guy acted as a mugger, he had to wear full protection, a metal body suit that was covered in padded, white canvas, which turned his body into something like a very mobile Humpty-Dumpty. Without telling me or anyone else, Mickey had colluded with one of the model muggers to get him to wear the mask. When the first mugger came at Charlene in the Humpty-Dumpty suit and the Tricky Dick face, the class broke into laughter. *This* was a good icebreaker. Before Mickey's prank, the women had been very nervous. (Doing your first totally improvised defense is always a little frightening.)

By the next-to-the-last class, when Mickey had not shown up for four weeks, I figured I would never see her again. I drove to Five Points a little slowly that day, and when I saw people walking along the streets, I craned my head out the window to see if one of them might be her. No such luck.

That night, as I started teaching, I heard a rumbling in the hallway. I ignored it for a while, but finally I went out. The hallway was dark, and I couldn't make out what was going on. There was a person so bundled up she looked as if she were wearing a Humpty-Dumpty suit. There were flashlights and reflectors strapped to her body, and there were several little bundled people all flashing with reflectors and flashlights, too. They were huddled around some kind of metal contraption. I said, cautiously, "May I help you?"

The biggest bundled figure turned around and the flashing lights blinded me. "Hey, Sensei," the voice said. It was Mickey.

"What're you doing? Where've you been?" I said.

"These are my kids," she said proudly. She introduced me to four kids, two boys and two girls. Their cheeks were rosy from the chilly weather, but they beamed as Mickey unbundled them. I looked at the contraption. It was an old clunker bicycle with a homemade trailer attached to it.

"Like it?" she said. "It's my Cadillac."

By now the other women had joined me in the hallway.

Before Mickey had a chance to unbundle herself, she was descended upon with a dozen embraces.

"What the hell, girl?" said Charlene.

"Long story," said Mickey. "But right now, can I just come back to class?"

Mickey's kids sat along the wall and played quietly. The class was far enough along that the other women could practice on their own, so I took some time to teach Mickey privately, helping her catch up.

"What's up?" I said as I taught her some grappling techniques and evasions.

"Oh, I had some stuff to take care of," she said. "It killed me to miss class though. I just—I didn't have a car, you know."

"You should have called the Y. I would have given you a ride. Anyone would have given you a ride."

"Oh, well, it was a little hard to get to my house," she said. "I was in jail."

I wanted to laugh, to believe this was a punch line. But something had happened to me between the first day of class and now. I no longer assumed that others' lives mirrored my own. It was an openness that came to me without judgment or expectation, as if the state of mind required for sparring was finally beginning to sink into my daily life. I said, "Why were you in jail?"

She shrugged. "Ran a red light."

Now I was surprised. "On your bike? C'mon!"

"Preposterous, huh? Well, I didn't pay the ticket for a million years, and then I resisted arrest." We were practicing a certain block, and her hand slapped the side of my punching arm over and over again with a snap. She exhaled sharply with each block, her eyes focused even as she spoke. "You see, I couldn't let them take my kids, and I knew they'd put me in jail if I didn't pay the fine. That's why I ran. I didn't pay it in the first place because I had to put my kids in day care. That's all the money I have for the month."

"So what *did* they do with your kids while you were in jail?" I said.

The blocks grew stronger, the slapping sounds and the exhalations steady as a train.

"Their dad," she said. "They stayed with him even though I came home one day, found him molesting my daughter. Police didn't do anything about that, no proof they said, but they had proof I ran the red light."

Unlike karate, all styles of Shao-Lin gong fu insist that the practitioner learn weapons: *kwun* (long staff), *sam gip kwun* (three-section staff), *dip do* (butterfly swords), and so on. In combination with the well-accepted history that credits the Buddhist monk, Bodhidharma (Da Mo) with traveling from India to China in about 500 C.E. and, once there, formalizing Zen Buddhism and the first movements that would eventually become Shao-Lin gong fu, there is the likely scenario of working-class peasants rising up against tyrannical Chinese governments. Some historians of gong fu believe that the art began first with weapons, and when the weapons were set down, the fighters found the movements they had performed with weapon in hand were equally effective with empty hands. This explains the sometimes odd-seeming gestures, the strenuous but powerful moves of gong fu.

In this theory of martial arts history, it was oppression that incited the beginning of gong fu. This is also the pattern of development seen in some more recently developed martial arts. Capoiera, for instance, is a deadly art developed by Africans who were brought to Brazil as slaves. After a massive uprising of slaves, the slave owners forbade the Africans to train for any sort of fisticuffs. Consequently, the Africans disguised their training as dance. Capoiera remains, today, a martial art practiced to music. Like other martial arts, it is sometimes difficult to see how it can be applied as self-defense; it looks like a beautiful dance combined with spectacular gymnastics. Once you spar a practitioner of Capoiera, however, you are left with no doubt about the art's martial efficiency.

This theory of how some martial arts may have originated ran through my mind as I drove home from that second-to-the-last class I taught in the inner city. I envisioned Mickey, Charlene, and the other women coming together to create their own style of martial arts. I saw them finding their own unique sense of power. Mickey was their fearless leader. They danced beautifully, and with rage.

≈

The following week, I had to say good-bye to my Five Points students for good. I usually ended my final classes with a bang, then ran home, paycheck in hand, happy to get back to what I loved the most: the *art* of martial arts, not just the self-defense. But at that last class with Mickey and Charlene and the other women, I hung around till nearly eleven o'clock, clarifying moves, answering "what if" questions, letting them throw me "one last time." We were like kids playing softball until the ball disappears in the dusk. When I could not hang around any longer without seeming a pest, I said good-bye, and my students walked me out. As I drove away, I saw Mickey lit up like a Christmas tree, towing her kids in that handmade trailer. I knew she had no place to go, but I knew, also, that among the limited choices available to her, she would choose what was best. She would survive. She had all the odds against her, and still, she would survive, even thrive. That's what I told myself as I pulled away, and a skinny knife of fear and nausea pierced my gut. I did not know if what I was telling myself as I drove away was the same "open-minded" positivity that I'd carried with me as my protection when I drove into Five Points to teach my first class. I wanted to believe that I had changed, that I had seen something real in these women, something that allowed them to transcend what seemed to be some pretty shoddy circumstances. Charlene had dropped out of high school but was now enrolled in a community college; another woman had been in a bad marriage and found her way out; the Asian woman had removed herself from an abusive situation. I believed they were fighters in the most real way, that they would transcend the circumstances of their lives.

It was an uncomfortable feeling, though, because usually I walked away knowing that I had given my students some usable tools. If they practiced what I'd taught them until the moves became second nature, they would be able to fend off many types of attacks—and, more important, they would have the self-esteem of *knowing* they were capable of standing their ground. To that extent, they would be empowered. But I wondered if my gift was secondary. I was, by the circumstances of my life, standing on the outside, looking in, with the power, always the power, to make the choice to walk away.

Rural

I was twenty-something and living in Taos, New Mexico, doing what people do for a living in Taos: working four jobs—ranch hand, graphic designer, kids' martial arts teacher, landscape laborer—just to stay afloat. I shared a house with two other people, and one day one of my roommates came home and said, "Seb told Sophie she was supposed to study martial arts with you."

Seb was short for Sebastian, the spirit who was supposedly being channeled through Connie-Francis, the wealthy woman who lived on the mesa and wore silk robes while she gardened. I said, "Well, I know Seb is a spirit, but here in the physical world, I don't have a place to teach Sophie martial arts."

That evening, I was at Connie-Francis's house. She was definitely a presence: five foot ten, hefty build, beautiful grey hair that she kept up in a loose bun, while strands fell to her shoulders like the tentacles of some tropical flower. Her voice was deep and resonant. After I demonstrated a few excerpts of external gong fu forms for her, we walked out onto the mesa, the sky so still a raven's call traveled for miles uninterrupted. I followed her down a red dirt path to a circular building with huge, curved picture windows all around it.

"We use this space about once a month for workshops." She swept her hand over the empty room. "The rest of the time, it's yours."

"It's beautiful," I said. "But how much is the rent?"

"No rent," she said.

I stumbled for words. "Well, will I need a key?"

"We never lock it. It's protected," she said, gliding away from me.

"Do you mind if I stay in the building, get to know the place a bit?" I called out to her.

She waved her hand, a corporeal thing emerging from the billowing cloud of her robe. "Take your time," she said.

I could never have afforded such a place. The curved walls had huge picture windows that framed the Sangre de Cristo Mountains on one side, the flat, open mesa on the other. The sun was just beginning to set, and the sky grew saturated with the deep reds of sunset until it was soaked to black, the stars like scatters of sunlight that could not bear to leave the sky. Forget the fact that the building had no mirrors, no mats, no hundred-pound bag. This was the place where I wanted to teach.

My roommate, the same one who had hooked me up with Connie-Francis, was the director of Parks and Recreation for the city. She said, "I'll reserve you a room in town, and you can do a demonstration. That'll get you some students."

I felt lucky. I posted flyers, and a week later, a conference room full of people attended the demonstration. By the end of the night, a dozen or so students had signed up.

≈

I began the class with various aspects of internal work, and for weeks on end we did nothing but meditate and breathe; there is no better way to build the self-discipline and patience necessary for martial arts. Plus, the place was right for it. We bonded as a group through the silence we shared.

After a while, though, Ginnie, the town rancher, started to get restless. She was a no-nonsense gal whose husband, a squeaky-clean dentist, had a strong dislike for earthy hobbies. But Ginnie could have been molded from the thick, sturdy clay that Taoseñas call *caliche*. She supplied most of the independent grocers with meat, milk, and eggs. I had helped her bale and buck hay on summer afternoons. When she called me up one afternoon and said, "It's here, it's here," I jumped into my beat-up VW bug and skittered down the rutted dirt road from the mesa to her farmhouse. There, I saw her out on the land, a slim, well-muscled woman in tight jeans and a blue gingham shirt, horses and cows milling around her as if she were one of them. She waved to me and hollered, "Come on in. Gate's open."

I pushed open the gate and ran out across the field. The sharp scent of sagebrush filled my nostrils. When I got there, I dropped to my knees and tossed my arms around a newly born calf, pink nose still wet from birthing, big brown eyes batting big brown eyelashes at the new world into which it had just, literally, been dropped.

"That's her," Ginnie said. "That's BK. I told you the next girl calf was gonna be named for you."

My arms still around the calf's neck, I looked up. "Since it's a she—" I said.

"She won't go to slaughter. Don't worry."

I breathed a sigh of relief. I had been at Ginnie's house for dinner before. She had served up hamburgers and jerky, saying, "This is Greg," or "This is Bruce," the names of two of my closest male friends in Taos. Ginnie had no tolerance for squeamishness. She took the world head-on, as it was, and while the other women in the class breathed into dan tien, Ginnie followed along, one eye open and laughing at the whole idea of qi. "When are we going to get to the good stuff?" she'd say.

To keep her interested, I started a round of applied self-defense. I would have started by showing my students how to use the everyday items they carried in their purses, but these women did not carry purses. I settled for my backup approach, to teach them a throw, let them feel what it was like to lift someone off the ground with little effort. I said, "Ginnie, would you like to try it on me? You can throw me full power; I know how to fall."

Ginnie stepped right up, though she pretended shyness. "Well, I don't know if I can do this," she said, knowing full well she could toss me through a window without so much as a day's martial arts training. She said, "I just grab here like this?"

"Yes, that's right," I said.

"And put my hip right there?"

"Yes, and bend your knees."

"Like that?"

"Exactly."

The second Ginnie understood what to do, I was off my feet, arcing my way weightlessly across the room, hollering out, "And remember, Ginnie, turn at the waist!"

I hit the ground, hard. Ginnie stood above me, looking down. "Is that close to right?" she said.

I nodded. "Pretty darn," I said. It was one of the best first throws I had ever witnessed. The other women lined up now, anxious to give it a shot.

≈

A few weeks later, I drove out to Ginnie's ranch to help her buck hay. When I arrived, she was sitting on the gate, cowboy boots hooked under the wood slats, chewing a blade of grass. Gazing up at the sky with her head tossed back, her blond hair shining in the sun, she looked as blissful as a high school girl after her first date. I called, "Hey, Gin, beautiful day, huh?"

It was unlike her not to hop off the fence and run to greet me. I kept walking, then climbed the wood slats and took a seat next to Ginnie. I let out a huge sigh (something about wide open spaces). I let my eyes rest on acre after acre of green sage and twisted piñon pine, Ginnie's ranch. Even from this distance, I could see where the earth dropped off into that deep gorge in the earth carved slowly and steadily by the Rio Grande. It was a sight I never got used to; I believed the Native American stories, that the gorge was the seam of the world, the place from which humans had emerged, rather than being dropped here from some distant place called heaven.

"You know," Ginnie said wistfully, "I think I finally understand what y'all are talking about when you talk about that qi hullabaloo," she said.

"Well, that's a shocker," I said.

She turned sideways toward me on the fence and hunched closer, as if telling a secret. "It just happened, I mean, I wish you'd a been here. I was driving the cattle inside the gate, and John, you know, my big bull, he was out of his pen. Well, he takes off running toward that open gate so fast I don't have time to think. I just swing off my saddle and throw myself at him, and so there I am, hanging from his head, like a rag doll. Right then, I started breathing, like you've been teaching us, right there into dan tien, and I'm hanging from the bull's neck, and then suddenly, I'm standing on the ground. I just kept breathing into dan tien, like you said." She shook her head in disbelief. "I'll be damned if that bull could not move me." Another shake of the head, more disbelief. "I pushed a running bull back into his pen. I felt this energy in my belly. Amazing. Qi, or some such hullabaloo."

She slapped my shoulder, hopped off the fence, and pointed to the baled hay we were due to buck.

SUBURBS

The houses were midsized and pristine. The neighborhoods had a calm, seething orderliness to them. There were stores— you know the names of them; there were stoplights, churches. There were one or two newly planted trees whose trunks were partially bound with tape and anchored to the ground with thick wire attached to tent stakes. This was so the trees would grow straight up and down, no unsightly crooks or bows.

The women's self-defense class I taught for the YWCA in the small, northern Denver suburb was held in a school gymnasium. At the first meeting, the women filed in, punctual and giggling. For some time, they hung out in the back of the gymnasium, waiting, until I called out, "Are you here for the self-defense class?" As if in an unbreakable huddle, they all moved closer to me at once.

I said, "Okay, let's get started. Let's see what items you might already be carrying in your purse that could be used as weapons."

After my experiences in the inner city, I always felt mildly voyeuristic doing this, seeing the lipstick tubes smeared with color, the wads of used chewing gum wrapped in foil; smelling the sudden scent of perfume mixed with cinnamon Trident. These women not only dumped their purses unabashedly, they rummaged through one another's piles.

"Oh, look at that!" Beth called, picking up one of Rebecca's many rat-tail combs. "I haven't seen one of these since the sixties. Now, that would make a good weapon, wouldn't you think?" She wielded it like a knife.

"Are those Safeway coupons?" Pat said. "I have been looking for Safeway coupons. They're doubles, aren't they?"

I had a hard time quieting them down so we could talk seriously about how to use what they were finding.

"Keys?" they said. "How about keys?" And they started gouging each other with their house keys.

I said, "Okay, okay, let's move on. Tonight I'm going to teach you a basic hip throw. Some judo." Now I had their attention. Though throwing a person is low on the list of preferred self-defense techniques, it's a good way to conjure confidence. I knew I'd lose their trust, however, if the first woman did not make the throw look easy, so I chose the boldest woman in the group. I said, "Beth, would you like to start?"

Beth swaggered to the front of the classroom. I illustrated how to step, how to lower her center of gravity. She took the lesson very seriously, said, "Mm hm, yes," as I gave instructions. The quiet in the room felt like a tennis match, or a golf tournament. In keeping with that oddly hushed mood, I found myself whispering instructions: "Now lift your hip and turn at the waist."

Beth lifted and turned, and in slow motion I tumbled over her back and landed on the mat. The silence shattered. The women gasped and laughed. Beth clapped her hands. "It's easy," she proclaimed.

But that was the end of easy. It took me the rest of the evening to cajole the other women into trying the throw once. As they finally stepped up, there was almost always a mock seriousness about them. For instance, when Barbara, a kind woman with frail wrists, stepped up, she furrowed her brow to an extreme. During the first step of the throw, the brow remained furrowed, the upper lip stiff, the eyes narrowed. She stepped in, grabbed my lapels, turned at the waist, and sent me sailing over her back, then onto the floor with a muffled thud. The minute I hit, however, Barbara's face took it all back. Her frown turned to a smile. Her stiff lip softened, and great surprise flooded her face. She held the flat of her palm against her cheek and looked at me lying there flat on my back. "Oh, Lord," she sighed. "Oh my." She knelt down to help me up. "I'm sorry. Are you okay? I am so sorry."

Her behavior did not surprise me. It was, in a nutshell, the general tone of nearly every self-defense class for women I had taught in the suburbs. Sometimes it took two full classes to get each woman to try the throw once. Each time I cajoled someone into stepping onto the mat, I had to act out a violent scene with great (if mock) gusto. Only then would they throw me—after which they would slip right back into laughter, shyness, proclaiming insistently, "Oh, I can't do that."

Gradually, however, the women quit giggling. As the self-defense grew more advanced and they began to feel the strength in their own bodies, they quit apologizing for that strength. They savored it, let it wind its way through their concept of who they believed they were. By the fourth week, they entered the room confidently, no longer huddled together. They arrived early and called me by my first name. They approached me with questions, supplied me with lists of techniques they wanted to learn, defenses against certain types of attacks. It was a transformation I had seen a hundred times, and each time it touched some familiar, if distant, part of me. The women, in a relatively short time, began to feel their bodies as something valuable, strong, potentially formidable—whether they were physically fit or not. In that sense, one self-defense technique sometimes seemed, to me, like a year's worth of therapy for their self-esteem.

Shortly after this growth spurt in self-esteem, the women in those classes began telling their stories. This was the sobering side of watching the thrilling transition. They opened up, and it was here that I learned their lives had not been easy, nor devoid of violence. Among them there had been rapes, domestic abuse, a child who had been abducted and murdered.

Here, again, I had to check my initial expectations at the door. Regardless of their positions in life, the locations of their neighborhoods, the amount of money they made, the women in the suburbs needed this self-defense as much as the women in the inner city. By the end of my time teaching these classes, I was no longer sure which was the greater myth: the safety of the suburbs or the violence of the inner city.

STEPPING OUT

It's a quirky habit of mine, a minor obsession. Sometimes I try to figure who I would be if I had been raised in another culture. I try to take my annoying individuality, my strong-willed American thought processes, my "leave me alone I will do it my way" attitude, and place it in modern-day China, or in some traditional Islamic culture where women can be put to death for making too much noise when they walk. I try to take off the cloak of culture, the layers and layers of what I believe to be me but is really only the set of circumstances into which I was born, and I try to grasp that popcorn kernel of what is unalterably me, my Self, my mind—my spirit, if you will.

Sometimes, I apply this odd little vision to others as well. I look out across the expanse of women to whom I have taught self-defense throughout the years. I can still see their faces, their mannerisms, the way they walked into class the first day, the very different way they walked out a few months later.

A friend of mine who is also a martial artist once told me he believes there is no way to *learn* martial arts, because learning implies acquisition. "Every martial art is a stripping away," he said. "They strip away expectations, limitations, delusions. They leave you with what is possible."

I think of Mickey riding her bicycle five miles a day to get her kids safely to day care and herself to work. I think of Fran, who could not do a single martial arts move on the first day of class without giggling and during the last class took solid charge in an impromptu situation.

I think of these things and I know what my friend said is true. Under the right circumstances, things fall away. Beneath them lies what has always been possible.

Five Is Becoming: A Meditation on the Nature of Qi

It is what separates martial arts from the category of pure sport or athletics. It is essential to all martial arts, but it is difficult to define. The nebulous quality of qi is what makes gong fu and karate seem mystical, or mysteriously powerful to those who have never practiced martial arts. The best definition of qi is the experience of qi.

Though qi has not been scientifically proven, neither has the mind. Although some scientists would argue that the brain *is* the mind, there is a general sense that mind transcends the brain. Certainly, there is no scientific proof for the unconscious mind, but much of the scientific community accepts it as fact. As mind is to the brain, so qi is to the body. An athlete who performs "superhuman" feats may be tapping into her qi; metaphorically, she could be using her body's "mind" (qi) in conjunction with her "muscles" (body).

A person may enter analysis and begin a process of bringing the unconscious mind into consciousness. Likewise, a person may enter martial arts (or any form of yoga), and begin the process of bringing qi into conscious use in the body.

A friend of mine who had seen a few gong fu movies that depicted martial artists flying was at first enthralled. After we spoke, however, she was disappointed. "I thought it might have been somehow possible," she said, "that flying." She is a very intelligent college professor and an accomplished rock climber. She believed it was perhaps possible to scale walls or to leap backwards into five-foot-tall trees. She said, "Well, I know there is *something* special about martial arts, but I don't know what it is. I thought that might be it. Flying."

Qi does not allow a person to fly. It does not allow a person to glide over treetops, to ward off bullets, or to slip one's body through solid walls. The cultivation of qi allows for something much more miraculous than all that. It allows one's body and-mind to be balanced, energized, healthy, calm. If you plan on frequently putting yourself in the pathway of flying fists (or other obstacles in life), healthy qi is essential.

Qi is the basis for Chinese medicine. It flows through the human body in fourteen main conduits called "meridians," but it also flows through every natural substance in the world, which is what the theory of feng shui is based on. To alter any natural substance is to redirect its natural flow of qi. To redirect the natural flow of qi through any substance is to redirect its natural flow of qi through the human body. Things connect up. We are a part of this world.

It's a dangerous thing to consider, the physical connection between our bodies and this world we live in, live with, and live off of. The discussion makes people nervous. If they are to be on the level with grass and beetles, they want definitions. They want proof. Qi, however, is difficult to describe in the English language. It's like trying to describe a brand-new color to someone who has never seen that color. It is entangled in Far Eastern languages, cultures, and world views. Without a common language, proof is nearly impossible.

Qi can be cultivated, stored, and directed, like electricity. Unlike electricity, qi cannot be measured in discreet units. At least, not yet. Institutes like the Menninger Clinic are currently researching this. Already, acupuncture, the purpose of which is to tone or strengthen unbalanced qi, is used in Western medicine. It has been used as an anesthesia in surgery procedures that require the patient to be alert during an operation. It has been used by dentists in place of a local anesthesia. If acupuncture works in these instances, and it does, and if acupuncture is based on the presence of qi, and it is, than there should be little doubt that qi exists.

≋

I was on a river trip in the San Juan canyon when the sky broke to rain. From the perspective provided by the narrow canyon walls, the horizon was hundreds of feet above my head. The clouds were even more distant than they appear on flat land.

Dark thunderheads moved across the skinny window of sky at the top of the canyon. They folded in on themselves, became heavy, and began to descend into the canyon. We (my friends and I) felt the walls of the canyon surging with thunder (the walls of our chests thrumming, too). For safety, we paddled our boats to shore. We sat on the banks of the river, craned our heads upward toward the brink of the canyon, and watched as lightning split the sky, striking the surface of the earth above.

Between the sky and river stood only a long, vertical stretch of immutable rock the color of sunrise. We sat in silence, the thunder resounding deeper and deeper. All at once, the lip of the canyon turned to mist and involuntarily, my friends and I gasped in unison. There were no words. The mist danced like an apparition for several seconds, a sheer veil of lace unfolding down the walls of the canyon. Then, as if pushed by a force, the mist coagulated. It formed a waterfall, and the waterfall cascaded toward the river, a white force rushing across the solid body of rock toward the fluid body of the river.

In the next few minutes, we watched waterfall after waterfall form. The earth above us was in a flash-flood.

This is one way to understand qi. It is everywhere, and at the same time, it coagulates and becomes the waterfall that informs the fluidity of the human body. When a person dies, that rush of qi disperses again. It returns, like mist, to the natural world. The spirit (qi) of a person is already and always eternal. Qi does not die; it only changes forms. Said Daoist master Zhuang Zi, "Every birth is a condensation of qi. Every death is a dispersal."

Odd numbers allow for continuation. Even numbers are whole, balanced, complete. Perhaps this is the reason that the basis of Chinese medicine (and the original Shao-Lin animal forms) come in packages of five. Five elements in acupuncture: wood, metal, water, fire, earth. Five internal organs: heart, liver, spleen, kidney, lung. Five directions: north, south, east, west, and center. Five original animal forms: crane, snake, tiger, leopard, dragon. The goal is balance, but the goal can never be fully attained. All things are becoming. Completion (exact balance, an even number) is death, which is not a bad thing. It is only a return. It signifies when you and your qi are done with this particular project.

Several types of qi circulate in human beings. The sum of all these is called *zhen* or Righteous Qi. When your Righteous Qi is flowing in a healthy give-and-take of yin and yang, you are healthy. To a martial artist, maintaining this give-and-take through meditation and controlled breathing is the same as a football player lifting weights. Strength, in martial arts, has a different foundation.

The internal organs are like constellations within the body: The kidney is the house of the will, or *zhi*. The liver is the house of the ethereal soul or *hun*. The heart is home to the mind and consciousness, or *shen*. The spleen is the house of the intellect, or *yi*. The lung is the house of the corporeal soul, or *po*.

The five main organs are related to the five main aspects of the human psyche. There is no distincion between mind and body, between body and earth. What is ethereal is tangible and what is tangible is ethereal. The human body is both.

≋

I am not nearly as accomplished in rock climbing as my friend who believed that flying might have been possible, that martial artists might have the ability to perform some limited form of the feat. I have, however, placed my hands in a few granite crevices and made a mad attempt to pull myself up the sheer face of a vertical cliff. The experience has made me understand how my friend believed weightlessness might be possible. Climbing, for me, was exhilarating, not so much because I was conquering anything or testing my will, but because the presence of the earth's qi was so evident when my hands were that close to something as raw and natural as an outcropping of solid rock. As I climbed, there were, indeed, times when I felt my body becoming incredibly light and agile. At those times, I could have sworn the rock turned to something fluid. I felt as if I were swimming up the rock, as if we (the rock and I) were moving together, that solid, immutable substance and my struggling, little body finally agreeing on graceful movement.

Science declares what is real and quantifiable. Each person decides for herself what is real and possible.

The best definition of qi is the experience of qi.

SECOND NATURE

During my college years (in my mid- to late twenties) when I lived in Boulder, Colorado, I had a routine. I awoke at five A.M., ran three miles to an outcropping of red rocks that emerged from the foothills like spines rising from the tail of a great, sleeping dragon. Once there, I stripped down to the bare essentials, a sports bra, shorts, no shoes, and I practiced qigong. I started, as usual, with the breathing exercises, and then I went into the internal animal forms ("frolics") founded by Hua Tuo (c. 110–207 C.E.), "the father of Chinese medicine." I performed the Crane, the Monkey, and, finally, began the Deer. By this time, I was in an altered state—not an altered state like I thought I was going to channel some ancient spirit or relive my past lives, but an altered state like any athlete or artist enters when she loses herself to her work. I stepped forward slowly, lifted my hands, looked over my left shoulder, as the form requires. I repeated the movement, the world around me taking on a kind of blur—which suddenly came into focus. In front of me stood a herd of deer.

It is not uncommon for deer to come dramatically close to you in the foothills of Boulder; they know they are safe, even though humans are everywhere. I noted them, and kept doing the deer form, which felt playfully enriched by their presence.

As I continued, however, the grazing deer moved closer and closer to me until, eventually, I was surrounded by them. The "lead deer" was no more than an arm's length away. I could easily have reached out and touched her nose.

It did not feel playfully enriching anymore. For a brief moment, I was utterly frightened. Deer are not predators, but they are wild. I once saw a film of a doe attacking a full-grown man; he did not fare well. Sometime earlier, I'd had to place myself between a mother deer and my dog, who had unwisely chased her fawn.

My fear waned, however, when I realized I had done nothing to threaten their territory. I had been here, moving slowly, sometimes standing very still, and they had come to me. If anything, they were encroaching on my territory—but I was all too willing to share. I relaxed and, as if they were not there, continued the form.

Before I finished the next move, however, I heard a strange sound. I am familiar with the birds of the Colorado foothills and can identify most of them by their songs. The sound I heard was a pinched sort of squeaking noise, like a nuthatch, but more drawn out than a nuthatch's peeps. It was connected, sustained, resonant. I continued the form, but I scanned the ponderosa pines and junipers for a migrant bird. When the sound came again, however, my ears led me back down to the ground. I looked straight in front of me and noticed the throat of the doe moving. I focused in on it. The noise sounded; the deer's throat moved, a direct correlation. Her eyes were looking straight at me, close enough that I could see the space between her eyelashes, the small notch cut out of her left ear in the shape of a tiny shark's tooth. She was moving toward me, slowly, making the odd noise as she approached.

Now I held just one position of the deer form because I could not really move any farther without virtually nuzzling the doe. I studied the sound; it came from way back in the deer's throat and was squeezed up through her vocal cords (though I did not know that deer had any vocal cords). Likewise, I squeezed the muscles in the bottom of my throat, and a sound that started in my diaphragm carried upward. I imitated the resonant squeaking the deer made. As the sound reached the doe's ears, she cocked her head. Her ears twitched. I did it again, and this time she responded with a sound that seemed the same pitch and length as mine. She added a few notes at the end, which I repeated back to her. She cocked her head, took a step or two closer to me, my heart pounding until she stopped. She was close enough to me now that I could feel her warm breath on my wrist. Again, she made the sound.

The other does had gone back to feeding, but they had not wandered far enough away to make me seem *other* than them.

So there I stood, completely still, in the middle of a herd of deer, carrying on what seemed very much like a conversation with a large doe.

≋

For fear of being committed to a mental institution, I haven't told many people this story. Before I arrived home, I was already discounting the event. I imagined myself in the woods, making noises back and forth with a deer, and I cringed. Clearly, and perhaps literally, I had lost my mind. While doing the internal deer form, I had been totally immersed in my body, and my body was immersed in my surroundings. Every movement of the form I was doing initiated in the soles of my feet, proceeded up my legs like a spring uncoiling, my torso turning and twisting like the ponderosa pines, their reddish roots spiraling to emerge from the sandstone rocks toward light. But as I finished the qigong and the deer departed, my mind came back from its brief vacation and settled into the throne it held over my body. Immediately, it began its harangue; it tossed New Age insults and edgy aspersions at my hulkish, gullible body that had stood unabashedly on a mountain and engaged in a verbal exchange with a deer. But in the midst of the mind's logical denunciations, my body said, "What about kissing?"

My mind shut up; it was stumped. It knows little of kissing because it departs as soon as the activity begins. Sure, there have been occasional, embarrassing moments when my mind has walked in on me in the middle of a kiss. Then all hell breaks loose (though I have to pretend nothing has upset the beautiful moment). I become uncomfortably aware that my tongue has gone to visit another person's tongue, and what an odd thing *that* is. There's that awkward exchange of bodily fluids, the strange little moans and smacking noises, the motion of the two muscular tongues wrestling, and, well, when the mind walks in unexpectedly, a kiss is *not* a kiss. There's no passion, no romance, no reason, no goal. Just the certain cognitive awareness that this activity is truly inane. But a kiss—unlike qi, unlike qigong, unlike talking to a deer—is a very American, socially agreed upon, tangible reality. Losing your mind to a kiss is a good thing. I shook off the incident on the mountain, let my mind take over, and began studying for the test scheduled in my Greek class that afternoon.

≋

I have never been enthralled with language as a means of communicating information—it's useful in that manner, yes, but it's a grocery list, nothing more. What I love about language is the way it wraps around something ineffable and makes it visible—and I don't mean through the use of imagery alone; I mean, also, through the word itself, the history it carries on its back, the way you mold it in your mouth, your mind.

That day, in class, I translated from Greek into English a line from *The Odyssey* that advises, "Keep the unspoken word in your heart" (I had opted for Fitzgerald's interpretation of the line). The word for "unspoken word" in Greek is *mythos*, the root of our word "myth," which meant, originally, simply "word" or "speech" but implied a subjective or poetic type of speech, perhaps something very real but at the same time ineffable. It sits in contrast to *logos*, the Greek word for "word" or "speech" that implies something purely rational, logical.

I don't know if it was the translation of that particular word and its meaning or if it was just the experience of entering another language and feeling the tenuous grip on reality that language, in its arbitrary precision, implies; but as I read the ancient Greek words, my perception of what had happened earlier that day began to change.

I sat there translating from Homeric Greek, a language neither I nor anyone else in our century had ever heard spoken truly accurately, and I was trying to capture the "sound of the original" in English, a language whose origins in me I could not remember but which had seemed to shape the world before I had a chance to comprehend that world fully, experientially. It presented in me a paradox that is perhaps all too theoretical and drab to reiterate here. The bottom line is, for whatever reason, as I entered another language my experience on the mountain earlier that morning was transformed. As far as I could tell, the deer had embodied a "language" at least as real as the language I was translating from the page. The experience I had so easily discounted replayed itself now. This time, it was not mind-bending. It was not extraordinary. It was what had happened. A deer had approached me. I had entered the ordinarily languageless space between humans and animals, and I had found there a sort of tenuous bridge. In the aftermath, in order to reshape my world into the comfortable distance I needed to live in the manner in which we have come to exist today, my own human arrogance convinced me that somehow all other life was incapable of language, and wouldn't I be silly to believe otherwise? That was the sensible thing to do, wasn't it? Because, as the philosopher David Abram has said, "when the animate powers that surround us are suddenly construed as having less significance than ourselves. . . then our sense of the wild . . . must migrate either into a supersensory heaven beyond the natural world or else into the human skull itself—the only allowable refuge, in this world, for what is ineffable and unfathomable."* My sense of the wild in my day-to-day life had, indeed, migrated. On the mountain that morning, it seemed it had returned home.

After my Greek test, I walked across campus to the museology department, where I knew the professor of dioramas and taxidermy would be able to answer the questions tumbling around in my roomy skull. I found him in the back of the museum with his hands inside a peregrine falcon's skin, so that his fists, from a distance, seemed ready to take flight. He was a quiet man, the kind who does not look at you when he speaks, and answers, usually, in a few syllables or less. I spent some time

---

*David Abram, *The Spell of the Sensuous* (New York: Vintage Books, 1997), p. 10.

admiring his work with the falcon, then I said, "Do you know much about mule deer?"

"A bit," he said. He nodded his head and lifted his eyebrows, betraying, unintentionally, that his answer was an understatement.

"Do you happen to know if the female deer ever makes a noise, you know, like, to communicate?"

He thought for a while. "She does, but you're unlikely to hear it. Why?"

"What kind of noise?"

He scratched his head. "A kind of garbled, high-pitched hum. In the springtime. To her young. You won't ever hear it."

A river rushed through my body. "Ever heard it yourself?" I said.

"Never did," he said. "But I know."

I said, "Thank you. Thanks very much."

I walked across campus, through town, and finally toward the red rocks where I had been earlier that morning. There, I let the world fold over me. I sat quietly, confirming what had happened, letting it take hold of my body as something that had happened, even if it was inexplicable—or perhaps *because* it was inexplicable.

After a while, I began doing qigong. I started with the breathing exercises, then followed with the internal animal frolics. As the sun dropped behind the red rocks and the sky turned inky blue, streaked with saffron calligraphies of clouds, I began doing parts of some external animal forms from different systems: Crane, Tiger, the dual form of Snake and Hawk.

The foundation for these movements had first entered my body when I was a kid, before I could "reason," so they and the effects they had on me did not seem esoteric or mystical to me. The feathered strength of the hawk's wings informed my arms; the cool belly of the snake's scales close to the earth informed my body, its slow recoiling, its quick strikes. I became the hawk spiraling down from the heavens ("Turning and turning in the widening gyre"), the snake coiling up from the earth, my body the conduit between the two (the falcon is one with the falconer). It is difficult to describe this in language that has not been appropriated by "New Age spiritualism" and its tendency to lift the most simple things from the most complex contexts; it is difficult to refrain from discounting it. But here, in this place, the center held. Here, things did not fall apart. I felt the "oral" tradition of movement, as it had been handed down through generations of gong fu practitioners throughout time. It felt the same as a poem feels when I take the time to read it and let the words become palpable.

I felt my body dancing in the way I had seen Sifu's body dance the first day I saw him, that magical figure in the darkness, the wildness in his body. It was part of what I loved about martial arts—the lack of self-doubt that comes with animal certainty, the sureness of movement, the reclamation of a language that exists in the body before it becomes words.

When I was done, I walked home along the river that runs through Boulder. On the way, I spotted a black-crowned night heron hunting. He stood perfectly still, all wing and eye, waiting. This, I thought, was the consciousness of the wild. Though it looks like patience, it is just abandoning your mind and body to a kiss.

≋

I think of the Shao-Lin monks and nuns, of the story that is told of them watching wild animals and creating, from those wild movements, the thousands of gong fu animal styles: snake, hawk, tiger, white tiger, crane, praying mantis, leopard, heron, even the mythic dragon, a style founded by the Shao-Lin nun Wu Mui, conjuring, as she did, the way an animal might move between the heavens and the earth, an animal fluid and change- able as clouds. This zoogenic aspect of gong fu is what makes it so versatile as a martial art. A good teacher who has knowl- edge of many different animal styles, for instance, can deter- mine which one might be best suited to a beginning student: the mantis, for a small, quick person; the tiger, for a strong, well-muscled person, and so on. In this way, each person learns to develop his or her attributes, leveling the playing field and the sparring ring. Likewise, an instructor can teach aspects of the tiger to someone whose innate tendencies are more "bird- like," thus helping the person find greater physical balance.

When I think of this aspect of gong fu, I wax romantic. I imagine the monks and nuns walking alone across the landscape of China, their brilliantly colored robes showing through the fog like the feathers of a bright bird. They must have sat for hours, days, months, simply *observing*.

As the story goes, the monk who watched the snake defend itself against the crane is the founder of the snake style of gong fu, and the one who watched the monkey ward off the tiger was the creator of the monkey style. But this explains only half the story—the self-defense half. It does not explain why every creature represented by the original Shao-Lin system also corresponded to a part of the human body: the tiger to the bone, the crane to the sinew, the leopard to the muscles, the dragon to the spirit, and the snake to the qi. It does not explain why each animal and each part of the body corresponded also to an element—earth, fire, water, air, metal—and each element to a direction, each direction to a positive (yang) or a negative (yin) force, each force to a season, each season to an emotion, each emotion to a sound, each sound to a taste, until, after many years of study, there was not a strand of experience left unaddressed by the weave.

Clearly what the monks and nuns were observing was far more than the fighting abilities of the animals that inhabited the world around them. They did not seek only to imitate the animals' movements; if that had been the case, they would have stopped when they applied the animal forms as self-defense. It seems, rather, they sought to find within themselves the delicate and complex balance they witnessed in the natural world. "Do you think you can improve on nature?" Daoist master Zhuang Zi wrote. "I do not think it can be done."

≋

I once read an essay by a surgeon who described his work as a semireligious experience. He felt awed and afraid every time he opened a human body to see the "untouched wilderness" there—a territory, like the most rugged wilderness, meant to be witnessed only by the gods. He described surgery as a justified "intrusion"; he entered the hallowed ground with compassion and the sole intent of restoring the body to its original state.

After years of martial arts practice and the intricate weave it threads between your flesh and bones and the world that surrounds you, you begin to feel this wilderness inside. Your body begins to feel like only an extension of the earth. In the beginning, this sensation, this extreme physical connection to the physical forms around me led me to take up other sports that, like martial arts, demanded intense focus and presence of mind. Through this state of mind, the world always seemed more crisp, the connection more indelible. I began rock climbing, white-water kayaking, and mountain biking as a complement to my practices of gong fu and qigong.

According to Chinese geomancy (on which the currently popular practice of feng shui is based), qi runs not only through the bodies of all living things but also through the earth itself.

I am not a person given to plunging into mystical theories, nor am I predisposed to exclude them just because they are not scientifically proven. Rather, my soul is bent toward language and images, and perhaps because of this, theories—whether mystical or scientific—come at me constantly as metaphor. When I began climbing the rock formations along the Rocky Mountain foothills, I learned that the area where I was climbing was called a "dragon line." Those sandstone and granite monuments that jutted from the softer flesh of the earth were, theoretically, plump with qi.

The story was uncannily like an image I had made up when I was a child. When I looked out my back door onto the mountainous horizon of the Front Range, I saw a sleeping dragon. The tallest mountains in the middle were the dragon's back, the spiny crags to the north were the dragon's tail, and the gradual slope to the south was the dragon's head. I imagined the dragon had gone to sleep thousands of years ago (a short time for a dragon, I thought), and I believed that if we harmed the dragon (or, as I used to say, if we were "mean to it") it would one day lift up off the earth, leaving a barren scar where the beautiful mountains had once been. Such was the way my child mind worked.

Now, as an adult, I was being told that this same stretch of land was called a "dragon line," and when that theory connected up with my study of martial arts and qi, I was bathed in metaphor, my most comfortable and invigorating state of mind. I wanted to get closer to those rocks, bury my hands in the icy cold granite cracks, and rely on the substance of that geology to cinch my hand tight enough and hold the weight of my body so that I would sometimes dangle hundreds of feet above the ground. A rock-climbing technique called a chimney was considered by most to be a "grunt"—that is, an ugly, difficult maneuver. It involved wedging your entire body into the space between two rocks (or the crack in one rock) and shimmying your way up. I had a hard time agreeing, however, that this move was a "grunt." Nothing felt better to me than the earth wrapping around my body like that, the jagged edges pressing against my stomach and spine.

I was drawn to a similar aspect of white-water kayaking. I had chosen to kayak rather than to raft because kayaking allows the closest proximity of the body to the river itself. There was the added candy of learning to read water, to determine, by the fluid patterns chiseled on the surface, what the earth beneath that river might look like. It was exhilarating and calming to be out, sometimes for weeks, reading water like language, moving at the exact speed of a river, in the exact direction of its current, my body shaken and tossed by the whims of the waves.

After only a few years of this, however, my vision of the world began to shift subtly. When, one day, I was standing on the edge of a cliff, looking down into the vast walls that hugged the northern New Mexico stretch of the Rio Grande, I felt swollen with rapture. I pointed to a wild part of the river, and I said, "That's Sunset Rapids, class five."

My friend had no idea what I was talking about. She said,

"You name things a lot, don't you." It was neither an insult nor a compliment, but for the rest of the drive through that canyon I noticed that I could no longer look at the world without placing a name on it. This section of rock became "the Diving Board," and that section, "the Naked Edge." It was like getting a song stuck in your mind and not being able to shake it loose, like when you're hiking in the wilderness and suddenly the commercial for Burger King starts playing in your head. It was something appliquéd from the outside onto my immediate experience. I didn't like it. I had the greatest urge to get out of the car right then and there, to hike down into that canyon and to take my place next to that river and do qigong and gong fu until my mind was cleared of all the crap running through it. It felt urgent.

It wasn't the naming in and of itself, however, that bothered me. To this day, I tend to savor the joy of learning the scientific names of indigenous wild plants and flowers, and the relative wilderness I experience on any hiking trip becomes richly textured by the songs of birds. It is important to me to know the names of those birds, to be able to hear their songs and, without seeing the animal itself, to know it is there, somewhere, within the weave of my immediate world. I need this sort of naming; it is accompanied by the intention of knowing the thing itself. That's what makes the difference. When I learned the names of certain routes on a rock, or the stretches of a river, my intentions were utilitarian; they seemed altogether too bound up in a sort of self-serving arrogance that comes too often with the combination of opposable thumb and ego. The name did not get me any closer to the thing itself, only closer to the way in which the thing itself would benefit my pleasure.

I don't know if this shift toward seeing the world through utilitarian eyes occurs in everyone who takes up outdoor sports. My guess is it does not. However, in me, it permeated my sense of the outdoors. It betrayed all that I had learned in martial arts—to observe the natural world as it is; to ignore the sense of ownership and use that accompanies ego. In stillness, I had learned to perceive. I had learned the external animal forms so long ago that their origins seemed as untraceable in my body as the origin of language in my mind. As I practiced a form, I listened to the underground pulse of rivers, the rush of blood in my ears as my heart pumped with the exertion it took to exact any form, any series of movements.

As I passed my prime for excelling at external martial arts, I turned to the internal arts—the animal frolics, the internal deer, for instance. Through these, I sought to continue the conversation I had been having with the natural world for so many years. The movements had become my second nature, my first access to understanding my body and myself as inextricable from the world around me.

After not seeing each other for some time, I met, again, one of my teachers, the renowned qigong master Ken Cohen, who had taught me the internal animal frolics of Hua Tuo, and the external Snake and Hawk form. When we first saw each other again, Ken said to me, "You have become more yourself. Mountains more like mountains. Rivers more like rivers." In that moment, I felt I had succeeded. In my mind, what Ken noticed in me is the ultimate goal of internal and external martial arts. Everything else is gravy.

In this sense, gong fu and qigong are a natural science of the self. They are purely a nature lover's "sport," perhaps more so, even than rock climbing or river running, both intimate experiences of the natural world, to be sure, but with some built-in distance (even if only because of the amount of high-tech equipment one must purchase to pursue these sports). The theory of martial arts does not utilize nature in any way but, rather, puts the practitioner on par with nature: no mountain to conquer, no wilderness to tame—only mountains as muscle, wilderness as heart, spleen, lung, the plate tectonics of the body, shifting, reforming constantly as tributaries of rivers run through it. Without this aspect of martial arts, you have only combat training or gymnastics—fine pursuits on many levels, yes, but not martial *arts*, at least, not gong fu, and not nei gong (internal Chinese martial arts in general).

I still visit the red rocks where I used to spend my early-morning hours when I was in college. The area around them has been made into a park now; trails wind easily up to the spires, and the rosy face of the sandstone is polka-dotted with fist-sized white circles, the spoor of climbers who have chalked their hands and scaled the most vertical channels of the rock. The marks there could have been left by me; I am not angry about their presence, nor am I resentful of the trails that have given easy access to humans and narrowed the habitat of the deer. Rather, I try to find the precarious balance between the intrinsic and extrinsic value of things—the beauty of the land as it is, the beauty of the land as it can be used for my (and other people's) pleasure. It is a difficult equation to tally, because, too often, use ends in depletion. To allow something beautiful to exist without our witness of its beauty seems antithetical to human nature.

Through martial arts, however, I have come to see that it is the presence of the wilderness inside my skin that tugs me toward seeking the wilderness on the other side of my skin. It's the same as a child seeking a like-minded friend, something, anything, to confirm her own most authentic existence. That, at base, is what martial arts lead to. That, at base, is what wilderness accomplishes. It conjures the willingness to let beauty exist without witness, without desire.

The deer I saw that morning moved like every perfection I had ever strived to attain, in martial arts or otherwise. Yet they were anything but "perfect." They just were.

Like anything wild.

Fighting Time

My body is mostly earth, mostly water and minerals I hold in common with other animals, the domestic dog and the beluga whale, the mountain lion and the sloth. Save for the way I love this life, the strands of days that glisten in my memory, the winglike appendages of seasons (leaf, rain, snow) that catch light and then fall to loss, the lips of my loved one that part so easily to a smile (encompass my heart), the voice of my mother, my memory of the age she once was arcing desperately to somehow comprehend the age she is now, the age she has become in the meantime, and the impending absence that awaits me, her absence (I brush it aside, until); save for the cinnamon-sweet smell of a fall evening, the musty scent of grasses moist with the first snow, the days that were once round narrowing to the squint of an eye, the wink of winter closing, the light it creates within its softened darkness, and the way it breaks, eventually, to spring, trembling, as it does, in the wake of its own beauty; save for these things and the way I love them, my body is happy being earth; it can comprehend returning itself to earth, closing its eyes to this place forever just as it comprehends the day-to-day substance of living, that particular celebration that goes on quietly as the night opens and closes and the seasons barrel headlong into one another, creating the sense of roundness that makes us whole. Save for these things and the way I love them, I could go without a fight into the necessary aging, the eventual and permanent silence between us all.

FIGHTING YOUTH

There are certain memories that, over time, become like dreams, not dreams, because of their sheer palpability. You close your eyes and they play again, the scents and sounds, the views you held back then, when you were younger. They are not nostalgia. They cause a certain discomfiture.

There is, for me, the time I was driving home from a week of camping in Moab, Utah. I drove at night to escape the desert's heat, and because I liked driving at night. I liked to watch the rose-colored monoliths, their human forms rising from the desert floor like a congregation of gods.

I passed through Utah in the darkness, and by dawn I was driving through a pastoral valley in Colorado where free-roaming cows occasionally lit up in my headlights, and the black road glistened beneath their hooves. On either side of the narrow road were small white houses. Their porch lamps were still glowing and everything was on the verge of morning. I stopped for a cow, and when it finally meandered from the middle of the road to the shoulder, my Volkswagen beetle sputtered forward, the engine making the only sound in that quiet break of day.

I was traveling the back roads, so I figured there was little chance of finding the caffeine buzz I wanted so badly. But as I rounded a bend leading out of the small town, a white stucco building appeared. Its walls were deeply cracked and the screen door waved slowly open and closed, though there was no wind. The word CAFE was hand-painted in blocky red letters that covered the entire side of one wall. Behind the cafe was a huge compound of white buildings connected to one another with gray ducts. A chain-link fence with *Danger, Keep Out* signs posted on it surrounded the place. Already there were people moving around in there, working. A sticky-smelling white smoke billowed from the compound's chimneys.

With my legs trembling and bright white circles flashing behind my eyelids whenever I blinked (the effects of all-night driving), I pulled into the dirt lot and walked to the cafe. When I opened the door, I saw half a dozen men sitting at the counter and a pot of coffee poised coyly on a warmer. I looked at it with desire. I said, "How much to fill this thermos with coffee?" The

skinny man behind the counter turned to look at me. The skin
on his face was thick and red, heavily scarred. The men at the
counter turned toward me in unison. As my eyes ticked down
the line of men looking at me, I saw that each one of them had
a distinctive mark—a scar, an extremity missing, an ear bloom-
ing red and raw from the side of his face. They wore the white
uniforms of the people who worked at the complex.

The skinny man pointed to the pot of coffee. "Sit a buck
on the counter," he said.

"Thank you," I said, and I filled my thermos, placed a dollar
bill on the counter, and left.

≋

It was a time in my life when I thought I would live forever, or
when, at least, the thought of dying did not portend so much
loss. I had yet to understand the human body as the rickety thing
it is, the rib cage suspended so precariously from the finger-
thin spine, each rib bending around the vital organs like a hand
folding around jewels (as if the hand could guard the value),
and the legs, with their poorly engineered, wobbly knees holding the teetering weight of the mighty torso. At nineteen, I did
not see the way the spine arcs from one pose to the next like the
stem of a delicate flower, the body designed, as it is, for beauty
rather than durability. My body still felt like a force with un-
limited potential. I believed I could drink that coffee and, if it

was full of contaminants and toxins (which I believed it probably was) from that odd complex behind the cafe, so what? *My*
body could fight things off, endlessly. *My* body was not suscep-
tible. That's what I believed. I had seen its resilience firsthand.
Didn't it spring back from punches and swiftly dodge powerful kicks? Hadn't it conquered insurmountable odds?

Confident though I may have pretended, the picture of the
men stayed with me, that sacred geometry of the human body
altered so grotesquely by, I assumed, some subtle violence that
had taken place in that huge plant where they all worked, their
need to make a daily wage—something they couldn't fight off.
It was my first glimpse into the sheer rudeness of mortality, to
see arms and legs so gruesomely altered, to see the calm acceptance on the men's faces.

FIGHTING AGING

This is what is happening in my mother's body and mind today.
Deep within her brain is a dark nugget of matter called the
substantia nigra. Its job is to create little packets of dopamine
and send them out to the basal ganglia, which open the package,
read the message, and then initiate movement in my mother's
body. The chain of command begins with my mother's will to,
let's say, bend her leg and take a step. Instead of things going
as they should, however, my mother's will lights the fuse that
runs to the substantia nigra and looks frantically for that little

package of dopamine, which it does not find because that dark place in my mother's brain is dying well before the rest of her body and mind is ready to do so. There is a very sparse amount of dopamine available, and so the spark scavenges what it can and then, dutifully, carries the incomplete message to the basal ganglia. The result is that the leg does not move, or it moves too much or too fast, or it spasms. In the face of this biology, there is no such thing as "mind over matter" (my repeated motto as a teenager). There is strength of will; there is persistence; but the mind and the body are one—and in the case of my mother, this mended dichotomy is not ideal.

She was seventy-three the day the doctor first said, "I notice a tremor in your left arm" and began the tests that, a week later, suggested she had Parkinson's. Now, at seventy-eight, she is nearly homebound, her body ravaged with a disease that has twisted her once delicate spine into something like a thick, gnarled oak. Her arms reach out for me with every step, her upper body bent forward and swaying constantly, as if trying to dodge invisible blows, a perpetual movement that ends at her hips, her lower body so rigid her feet have become anvils weighted to the floor, nothing like the roots of a tree (the fighter is nothing without footwork).

Occasionally she says to me, "They don't even know what causes Parkinson's. How can they know I have it?" Her reasoning is as illogical as the disease, but the first part of the equation is true. Parkinson's is "idiopathic," the cause unknown. Certain causes, however, have been ruled out. In "typical" Parkinson's (when the symptoms appear after the age of fifty) genetics are *not* the cause of the disease. According to a report published in the *Los Angeles Times* (and every other major newspaper) in January 1999, "That leaves environmental chemicals as the culprit for the vast majority of Parkinson's. . . . In announcing their results, [scientists] specifically pointed out that the search for causes of Parkinson's should now refocus on environmental chemicals such as fertilizers, pesticides, and herbicides."

If you watched me with my mother for a day, the way I comb the hair around her face, the way I stand with my legs balanced on both rims of a bathtub and, with my comparatively slight body, lower her into the warm water, joking with her all the way, listening to her laughter, the way she jokes back with me until she sinks into the comfort of the bath, sighs, and I massage her scalp with shampoo, my clothes soaked from chest to ankle, my heart pounding with exertion, sadness, fear, if you saw these things, you would likely not see the rage that informs my every move.

I have pictures of the home where I was born. In one of them, my mother and father are wearing shorts and T-shirts, leaning on snow shovels, and smiling like monkeys at the camera. Their feet are swallowed to the ankle in a fine dust that drifts, graceful as snow, against the rose hedge that borders our newly landscaped, heavily fertilized yard. Behind them, you can see all the way to the Front Range of the Rocky Mountains. You can see the distinctive outlines of Eldorado Canyon, whose rock walls embrace one-hundred-mile-an-hour winds that blast through and at the mouth of the canyon, bloom low across the open plains. As those winds barreled across the open plains back then, they picked up debris and the first layer of recently farmed, heavily pesticided earth, rolling it like a massive carpet until it reached our neighborhood, where it accumulated in drifts against hedges, fences, the sides of our homes. The families there, mine included, ogled the wonder of wind, the speed and power made visible in the mounds of dust we brightly shoveled. The dust brought with it a real social affair. It was a reason for many families to work outside, together.

Between Eldorado Canyon and my childhood home there was not a house or an apartment, not a gas station or a Wal-Mart. It was, as I said, only farmland, with the quiet interruption of a few stoic, industrial chimneys. They stood erect, just below the mountain horizon, rising from a complex of buildings about which we knew little, except what my father, a career military man, told us. He said, driving by the complex one day, "This is the place where they build atom bombs." He smiled. "Right in our backyard!" He said it with such glee and importance that sometimes, as a child, I was moved to walk out into the endless, open fields behind my house and push my way through curtains of tall grass and cattails until I could see the narrow smokestacks rising, immutable as the mountains behind them. When I was six, I would stand there at attention, believing the mountains and the chimneys were equal in power and beauty.

I was looking at Rocky Flats Nuclear Weapons Facility, ten miles or so upwind from my backyard. The waste from that facility, too, was a part of the dust that rolled across the land and accumulated in our backyards, the dust we shoveled so merrily, content and privileged, as we were, to be able to live our day-to-day lives under the splendid Colorado sky.

These are the memories that enter my head as I bathe my mother. I run the sponge down her spine, noting the way the vertebrae bulge distinctly, like a row of garden rocks tucked just underneath her first layer of skin, curving this way and that, each curve cupping a mound of spasmed muscle. "I have bones sticking out of my back, not my spine," my mother says curiously. She believes the hip replacement she had a few years back has floated to the surface of her body; she can feel the metal protruding, she says. I have not been able to convince her that the bone and metal she feels are her muscles, once supple and strong, made rigid as steel by the disease inhabiting her body.

I've grown to realize that what comes naturally is either this, or that; either the nostalgic images of my mom as a young woman working and playing in my childhood home, or the very vivid picture I see of her now, her body bent, her mind struggling to form words, to laugh. I try to conjure the mother I knew only two years ago, the one who was aging gracefully, enjoying her elder years, working out at the gym, gardening, swimming with her group of lady friends who were so dedicated they went to the outdoor pool even during the first light snows of winter. On my way to visit my mother I sometimes see them, their transistor radio poolside, the group of them keeping the beat of the music, singing as they work out. My mother is not among them, and I can't get a picture in my mind of her ever being among them; the memory has become theory.

It is, I think, the brain's way of forcing acceptance, the present bridging to a distant, golden past, with nothing in between, no direct access to yesterday or last month.

It happens to me also with the land (my body is mostly earth). Though my childhood and the ground I walked then seem so vivid—the detailed scents of summer, the way birds flew up in bunches and turned all at once, like a living cloud exhilarated by sky—I can't recall, in detail, the hills I walked a year ago, the same hills that now lie beneath the new mall. Though I spent the past five spring seasons watching a pair of mated bald eagles fledge their young in a tree that stood where the food court is, I can remember it only abstractly. The place seems as if it has always been as it is now, food court for eagle, and my mother's body seems always to have been crooked.

It is this gap between golden nostalgia and the present time that makes loss palatable. I struggle to suture the gap and restore what I know to be true.

I struggle to close the distance, sometimes, even in myself. Throughout my life I have studied with many good martial arts teachers. Partially through them and the movements they taught me of deer and hawk, of tiger and white crane, I have come to feel inextricable from a weave of life that envelops me in history and the natural world. I recall Sifu's voice, repeating to me the phrase that, these days, has become a cliché (though it was nearly sacred to me then): "Become the animal," and now, "Become the tennis ball," "Become the guitar"—become that which you seek to master. It is used mostly in a light, mocking manner. But the superficiality of pop culture does not change what has been true of martial arts for centuries: there is no way to master a form unless you become not only the animal but the earth beneath the animal's feet, the elements within which the animal lives—water, metal, air, fire, earth—and the seasons, the sounds, the emotions, the parts of your own body related (in Chinese medicine and martial arts) to the essence of that animal. Unless your body becomes inextricable from the earth and all that surrounds it, you will succeed only superficially. You may be a good fighter, or you may perform visually pleasing forms. But the whole of martial arts provides a weave that, unlike Penelope's cloth, cannot be done during the day and undone during the night. Gong fu has been the background of my life from such an early age that it is impossible now for me to separate myself from that which surrounds me.

My ability to practice external martial arts was challenged, however, when I was in my mid-thirties. In the span of a few years, my body (the same one I believed would live forever) went haywire. My endocrine system, which doctors define as "the time clock of the body," turned on and off on whim. My adrenal glands were working overtime just to keep me awake, and a cup of coffee caused me to drop into a deep sleep. In my mid-thirties, and without explanation, I was postmenopausal, but at the same time, my body was acting as if it were carrying a child. Doctors were befuddled. The menopause was irreversible, they said. As a result, they told me, my muscle tone would decrease. They warned me of fatigue, loss of memory, and premature osteoporosis. They projected the likelihood of early aging.

In addition to seeking the help of Western doctors, I had regular treatments from a doctor of Chinese medicine in San Francisco's Chinatown. The Chinese doctor charged me ten dollars per session, and each session varied from fifteen minutes to over an hour. He held my wrist in his hand, taking the pulses of my qi meridians; then he scrawled some Chinese words on a pad while his wife hand-chopped herbs, weighed them on an ancient scale (the kind of scale used as an emblem of justice), packaged them in large bundles, and handed them to me. The cost was three dollars. When I asked the doctor what the diagnosis was, he shrugged as if I would not understand.

I said, "I know a little bit about Chinese medicine. Can you tell me the Chinese diagnosis?"

As he was taking notes, he said, "The wind enters your body." That was it. *The wind enters your body.*

This was similar to something I had heard before, from Sifu.

It was taboo, according to him, to practice internal or external martial arts in bad weather. It was important to always practice in a warm, well-ventilated place, free of wind, drafts, and extreme dampness. For a man who appeared so tough and so demanding of himself and others, this seemed to me a contradictory behavior. I ignored his eccentric warnings. I sometimes practiced outside in the pouring rain, "toughening" myself up. If I was teaching a martial arts class and I had to go from the kwoon to my car, I did not put on shoes, even if four feet of snow covered the ground. I liked to face this kind of easy adversity. Sifu's tenderfooted approach to weather puzzled me. He did not disdain wind and rain; he simply bundled up to protect himself from them.

Although the language barrier between the doctor and me was even greater than the one I shared with Sifu (the doctor spoke Cantonese, and I had learned only a bit of Mandarin from Sifu), I struggled through. I said, "I don't understand why I'm having all these problems. I've practiced my martial arts diligently. I've done all kinds of nei gong."

The doctor replied crossly, "You think you practice nei gong it make you superman? The nature world outside is bigger than you. Out of balance out there, out of balance in here." He tapped my wrist.

His statement helped me understand what I thought I already knew: internal martial arts and acupuncture are designed to balance and heal the body. In doing so, they also recognize a give-and-take between the human body and the natural world. Unlike Western approaches, they are not really designed to *conquer* the ailments of the body so much as to return the body to a more natural state—whatever that state may be. This process is always healing, but it does not always cure. The bottom line is, if our environment is out of balance, our bodies will increasingly reflect that damage. We cannot separate environmentalism from our personal health. Although there have been documented cases of cancer going into remission after several months of qigong practice, there is no way to measure all the variables that may contribute to such remission. Due to my experiences with qi, however, I believe that the practice of qigong likely plays a significant role in such cases. On a more quotidian level, however, I know that qigong enhances the quality of one's daily life, whether battling an illness or enjoying perfect health. It's not a small thing.

In my case, traditional Western doctors were surprised to the point of fearing a lawsuit (something that never crossed my mind) when, after I increased my practice of qigong and other internal martial arts for a year, they tested me and declared my "irreversible" condition reversed. This diagnosis came from the result of their own lab tests. My FSH (follicle-stimulating hormone) level went from 100 to 18, the reverse direction FSH levels are supposed to travel during menopause. The reversal was only temporary; but it allowed me the time (a few years) to accept the changes that had previously taken place in a few months.

≋

By this time in my life, I had begun a career as a teacher at the college level. Sometime after I began practicing qigong more diligently, I was at work, teaching a freshmen-level class on comparative mythologies. I realized as I spoke that, though I was all American (how could I be anything else?), I had lived half my life with my face pressed against the window of another culture, looking in. I was like a child peering into a magical but unreachable world. Given my distance, I had the luxury of selecting only the positive aspects of Chinese culture. I longed for that world, and when I turned from that window back to the world in which my feet were planted, I felt somehow separate from my own culture. It had caused a chasm in me that I now longed to mend.

On the one hand, the American in me wanted to push myself to every physical and mental limit my body and mind tried to set up. I wanted to reach those limits and to surpass them, to "be all that I could be."

As I taught my class that day, however, I began to see how uncreative that behavior was, how it lacked any real discretion. I was acting out only the most palatable and mainstream of American ideals. By combining the rigors of martial arts with the attitudes of my own culture, I had turned my relationship with my body into a Jeep commercial. I was splashing through rivers, braving the wind and rain, thumbing my nose at the snow. My body and its off-kilter endocrine system, however, were teaching me that slowing down was exactly what deepened martial arts in a person.

Before this time, I had been allowed the privilege of letting the balance demanded of martial arts exist, to one extent or another, as a mere theory inside my head. This is why I could not understand Sifu's apparent hypervigilence regarding the elements. Now, however, I was glad to embrace Sifu's tenderfooted approach to weather. It elicited a greater awareness in me of the natural world as a whole, its power, its grandeur. As I increased my qigong practice, I could feel my body and mind balancing even deeper than they had before, when my training was heavily weighted toward the external marital arts. It was a state of mind and health that I welcomed. Just as Sifu had said, I did not feel as if I were slowing down. Even though my health had been temporarily compromised, I felt stronger, more whole as a martial artist and a person.

If the body, however, is inextricable from its surroundings, there is more to the story of one's health than lifestyle and genetics. I am haunted by the fact that pesticides, in their early days, were called "endocrine interrupters." I am angered by the fact that, according to the scientist Sandra Steingraber, popular literature on cancer tends to overlook the World Health Organization's report that states "at least 80 percent of all cancer is attributable to the environmental influences." In this study, the word "environmental" refers to "everything we interact with or consume that is *not* freely chosen." It is placed in contrast to "lifestyle," which refers to "that which we choose to consume: breathing air as opposed to eating dessert, drinking water as opposed to dipping snuff."* I want to be able to fight effectively when I read that "cancer rates continue to rise sharply and a flood of synthetic, hormone-mimicking chemicals continues to exert wide-ranging effects on people and wildlife,"+ but I'm uncertain where and who my opponent is. I am bothered by the reality that radiation causes a breakdown of the immune system, and that many odd, "new" health conditions (like the one that affected me) have their roots in exactly these: the breakdown of the endocrine and immune systems of our own bodies.

I am further bothered by the fact that the girl who was my best friend as a small child developed, in her early thirties, the same "idiopathic," multifaceted symptoms I developed: premature ovarian failure, substantial adrenalin loss, and the breakdown of the immune system. We were, by then, living worlds apart from each other, connected by memories we held dear, unaware of any subtle violence combing our bodies.

I worry that when health ailments befall us, we often be-

---

*Sandra Steingraber, *Living Downstream* (New York: Randon House, 1997), p. 60–61.

+David Ehrenfeld, "Pretending," *Orion Magazine*, Autumn 2000.

lieve they are either "our fault" or "our fate." But this is part of the imbalance. It is what allows us to push the limits of the land (our bodies) and to overshoot our natural resources (our bodies).

Out of balance out there. Out of balance in here.

It is empowering to believe we can stay in good health by making the right choices in lifestyle. It is equally empowering, however, to realize that these choices, to a large degree, also extend to the natural world, the environment. Paying attention to lifestyle and genetics means little unless we also find the strength to fight against the degradation of that environment, to be aware of the imbalances forced upon it, to be sensitive to the balance we are effecting with every choice we make.

FIGHTING INNOCENCE

Three months after I was born, a massive fire struck the Rocky Flats Nuclear Weapons Facility. Firefighters made many attempts to extinguish the blaze with carbon dioxide. The attempts failed. The fire burned through the night. Bits of plutonium, a pyrophoric substance, danced above the mountain horizon like giant sparklers rising through columns of black smoke. Toward the early-morning hours, firefighters gave in to an action they had tried to avoid, and some thirteen hours after the fire began, the facility and several hundreds of acres of earth were saturated in water, used as a last resort to douse the blaze. Although officials assured the public that any escape of the highly carcinogenic plutonium into the atmosphere was negligible, "there was no reliable equipment operable at the time to monitor the amount of radiation that actually went out the stacks. Not until a week after the fire were working gauges installed. Then, in a single day, emissions registered sixteen thousand times the permissible level—a full fifty years' worth of the allowable quota."[*] No one addressed the contaminated water as it began sinking into the local water table.

This was the first of several major fires at Rocky Flats.

Twenty-odd years after that first fire, I sat on the ground outside the high-security fence, listening to Bonnie Raitt, Daniel Ellsberg, Dr. Helen Caldicott, Jackson Browne, and many others. They had gathered on a makeshift stage to draw attention to the plant's dangers. Rocky Flats, they warned, was the only nuclear weapons facility that had been built in a residential area. In addition to this, records indicated that levels of airborne plutonium were higher at Rocky Flats than in any of fifty other U.S. stations. Dust samples downwind of the plant showed plutonium concentrations 3,390 times what might be expected from fallout.

---

[*]Harvey Wasserman and Norman Solomon, *Killing Our Own* (New York: Dell Publishing Company, 1982), p. 261.

What the residents (my family and friends) around Rocky Flats Nuclear Weapons Facility knew was that the plant manufactured "triggers" for nuclear bombs; what we didn't know was that the word "trigger" was a euphemism, conjuring, as it does, the simple metal piece hanging from the grip of a gun. A nuclear trigger, however, is the gut of a bomb, a hockey puck–sized disk loaded with enough plutonium in and of itself to effect a blast the size of the bomb dropped on Hiroshima. (Placed in today's sophisticated weapons, this trigger would effect a blast six hundred times that magnitude.) Rocky Flats, the facility in my "backyard," as my father proudly pointed out, manufactured somewhere in the neighborhood of seventy thousand of these nuclear triggers before it closed.

Currently, at Rocky Flats, workers are seeking a way to clean up the place and transform this tainted ground into six thousand acres of "hiking trails." Some problems they are facing: to find a way to drain some 4,060 gallons of plutonium solutions from leaky pipes and tanks (they have been leaking into the soil for decades); to locate approximately 1,100 pounds of plutonium that was lost in the ductwork during production (this is enough plutonium to create 150 bombs like the one dropped on Nagasaki); to clean thirteen "infinity" rooms— rooms that, when tested for radiation, cause the instruments to point to "infinity" on the gauge. In the process of accomplishing all this, they must move sixteen thousand pounds of high-grade plutonium through Denver and across the country to South Carolina.

I wonder who will hike the trails when they are completed, if the interpretive signs will tell visitors they are walking only a few feet above infinity.

FIGHTING TIME

As I have been writing this book, the latter part of fall has been turning to winter. I sit at my desk, and I look up toward a window that opens to the world. There are times when the light blazes through so harshly that the letters on the screen of my computer disappear in the glare. I keep typing, and as my pupils are soaked to black, full of light that blinds me, I see, occasionally, the silhouettes of hundreds of Canada geese flying overhead. Their heavy, winged bodies intersect the small window in a geometry of flight that flickers like a candle, its flame nearly out, then surging, the wings of the wild birds bending, extending. When this happens, I sometimes stop writing and go out. There is a small parcel of land behind my home. It is not *my* land, but there has been little else in my life that seems more like something that cannot be taken from me. Others might look at it and believe it is a pitiful thing, but I love it dearly. It is some fifty acres of tall grass and weeds, a pond, some cattails, and the dusty, lunar-landscape-like mounds of a prairie dog village. I stand there, and as the Canada geese cross the sky, the sun goes out for a moment, in the same way it darkens and chills when a heavy cloud passes. The sound of the geese falls around my ears like jazz. I can hear not only their nasal honking, not only the brush of their wings through air, I can also hear the creak of their joints as their wings pump up and down. I allow myself to fall into the sheer stimulation of every one of my senses: my eyes full of flight; my nose full of damp, snow-melted grasses; the wind touching my skin like fingers; my ears selecting the specifics of sound; my voice a laughter I cannot hold back.

Recently, I have learned that a developer wants to turn this land into a plot of convenience stores. Although martial arts have taught me how to walk away from a fight, they have also taught me that sometimes you cannot walk away. For me, now is that time. I have organized an active grassroots alliance to fight this and other unnecessary developments in our community. We attend City Council and city planning meetings. We set up educational booths in stores and on street corners. We pester city officials to allow open spaces to remain open spaces. So far, we are winning. It's not that we abhor convenience. It's that we feel slathered in it. It no longer feels like a privilege; instead it is a burden, like something so heavily out of balance that it has invaded me, the body I have sought to care for and whose balance I have finally learned to maintain.

One of my teachers once told me that one goal of martial arts is to learn to love the world with all your might and, when the time comes to let it go, to let it go; however, I have never reached this ideal. It still gets under my skin, this world. I want the imperfect grace of it all to pour over me; I want to swoon when I see beauty, to cower when I feel fear, to remain strong enough to allow every emotion to weaken me. I want to wrap myself around these moments, squeeze them for their beauty, their grace, their ugliness, their sorrow.

At night, when I fall asleep, I sometimes imagine the backhoes digging into the fleshy hip of that land. They are superimposed on the image of my mother's ravaged body, bent and torn by a disease whose cause was preventable, but not by her. Although I know the natural world may continue to renew and restore itself without my intervention, the fight I feel in my bones is not only about restoring the natural world. It is about healing myself, my loved ones. I feel, sometimes, overwhelmed by the vastness of it all, by a momentum outside my body that seems, periodically, unfathomable. Then I remember that I know what it takes to fight a good fight. I know that rage must fade away and give itself up to a steady, constant compassion, a focus not on what I choose to fight against but what I choose to fight for, to cling to, to love. Because sparring, doing forms, meditating, they all share in common the incredible strength it takes to move from one point to the next with as much clarity, integrity, compassion, and unmitigated intention as possible. They have created, in me, the simple ability to stay the course, to know when it is necessary to fight, and when that time comes, to fight with the soft and fluid stillness of a river.

ACKNOWLEDGMENTS

If the stories in these pages indicate I have sometimes put up a good fight, please know that any match I ever entered into was a cakewalk compared to my mother's daily fight against Parkinson's disease. Any amount of will, strength, self-discipline, or compassion I may have developed throughout the years has its foundation in her. Thanks also to my sister, the gifted ballet dancer who taught me early on how to move my body with grace.

Though editors are sometimes slipped in near the end of the acknowledgments section, Enrica Gadler, from The Lyons Press, sits at the top of my list. Her kind suggestion is what brought me to write about my experiences in martial arts in the first place. For her tremendous insight, undying enthusiasm and support, and her friendship, I am grateful.

I also owe many thanks to H. Emerson Blake and Aina Barten of *Orion Magazine*.

The cover of the book would not have a river running through it had it not been for the hours of work donated by my dear friend—and an extraordinary artist—John Dziadecki. May you one day fly in the illuminated dirigible of your choice.

A special thanks goes out to my friends and enthusiastic readers, Dana D., Lynne Lowry, Lisa Antosofsky, Donna Garbarini, and Leslie Ahr. Thanks especially to Susan Fox Rogers for being the best cheerleader anyone could be without donning a pleated miniskirt, and to Susan Feniger for saying, at numerous dinner gatherings, "Hey, tell that story about the time you sparred against so-and-so again!" She listened then, and she still acted interested when she read the same stories in the manuscript. Thanks also to the writer Liz Lachman for her close attention, intelligent feedback, encouragement, and valued friendship. I offer lavish gratitude to Lisa Cech, my own private editor and an unsuspecting Daoist master.

The profound appreciation I have for my many martial arts teachers and students (who are also my teachers) throughout the years spills over the limits of this page. Please know that I continue to learn from all of you, even in your absence. Thanks also to my most recent teacher, qigong master Kenneth Cohen, whose balanced, compassionate teaching and continually expanding knowledge is unparalleled today.

With deepest gratitude to the Bubo. You will remain.